DISASTER SURVIVAL 101

Adams Media
An Imprint of Simon & Schuster, LLC
100 Technology Center Drive
Stoughton, Massachusetts 02072

First Adams Media trade paperback edition December 2024

ADAMS MEDIA and colophon are registered trademarks of Simon & Schuster, LLC.

Simon & Schuster: Celebrating 100 Years of Publishing in 2024

For information about special discounts for bulk purchases, please contact Simon & Schuster Special Sales at 1-866-506-1949 or business@simonandschuster.com.

The Simon & Schuster Speakers Bureau can bring authors to your live event. For more information or to book an event, contact the Simon & Schuster Speakers Bureau at 1-866-248-3049 or visit our website at www.simonspeakers.com.

Interior design by Sylvia McArdle
Interior images © 123RF
Photographs by Creek Stewart unless otherwise noted

Manufactured in the United States of America

1 2024

Library of Congress Cataloging-in-Publication Data has been applied for.

ISBN 978-1-5072-2307-9
ISBN 978-1-5072-2308-6 (ebook)

DISASTER SURVIVAL

101

THE ESSENTIAL GUIDE TO
Preparing for—and Surviving—
Any Emergency Scenario

CREEK STEWART
Author of *The Disaster-Ready Home*

ADAMS MEDIA
NEW YORK   LONDON   TORONTO   SYDNEY   NEW DELHI

CONTENTS

INTRODUCTION

We live in an unpredictable world. From natural disasters such as hurricanes, wildfires, and floods to active shooters and grid failures, the risk of disaster affects us all. *Disaster Survival 101* will help you and your family make critical preparedness decisions before, during, and after a crisis. You will learn why, when, and how to effectively make decisions concerning sheltering in place, implementing evacuation procedures, and navigating dozens of specific disaster scenarios.

In this comprehensive guide, you will find both simple and actionable strategies not only to handle crisis situations but also to become more self-sufficient. You will learn how to make clearheaded and informed decisions about whether to *stay* or *go* in a disaster situation and what steps to take in either scenario to protect you, your family, and your home. This book will equip you with the essential tools, solutions, and decision-making mindset to safely and effectively navigate any disaster thrown at you. You will discover:

- The importance of risk assessment, especially before disaster strikes.
- The basic principles of disaster and survival preparedness.
- Strategies for making your home disaster ready.
- How to be prepared in critical shelter-in-place categories like food storage, water supply, heating, power generation, communication tools, essential first aid, and self and home defense.

- Clear decision-making tools for determining when and how to safely evacuate and how to build a 72-hour disaster survival kit (bug out bag) to provide essential survival necessities during evacuation.

This book also includes a part featuring twenty-three of the most likely disaster scenarios to happen and how to assess their immediate risks and threats. You'll learn how to make critical survival decisions such as whether to stay (shelter in place) or go (evacuate to a safer destination)—and fast-action checklists for whichever option you choose.

Because preparing for disaster situations can be overwhelming at times, *Disaster Survival 101* can work for you on several levels. First, you can use this book as a reference and checklist to identify small, manageable projects in your preparedness plan that you can methodically complete. Second, the book works as a day-to-day preparedness manual and is a great place to take notes on what areas of your disaster plan need work. Remember, this guide isn't just a resource to help prepare in advance of disaster. It's also a tool to help you make quick and informed decisions *in the midst* of a crisis. Keep it at the ready.

Disaster Survival 101 is designed to empower you to take action in crisis situations by the way it presents the material in a commonsense, nonsensationalized manner that reduces overwhelm, builds confidence, and encourages action. Remember, it's not IF but WHEN!

PART 1

UNDERSTANDING DISASTER PREPAREDNESS

Disaster preparedness can be overwhelming. It encompasses dozens of topics, countless different scenarios, and infinite combinations of circumstances. Just figuring out where to start can be a hurdle that stops some people in their tracks.

The first part of this book is designed to help you build a foundation from which to work. You will start by defining the scope of disaster preparedness as it relates to protecting you and your family in uncertain times. From there you will conduct a thorough personal risk assessment to identify your weaknesses and vulner-abilities. These will be specific to your life, your circumstances, and the most likely disasters to happen in your area.

It is only after you have identified your vulnerabilities that you can begin to chip away at implementing solutions. This first part is your road map for action. By the end you'll have a checklist of issues that you will need to address in order to be more resilient, prepared, and self-sufficient when disaster strikes.

CHAPTER 1

THE NEED FOR PREPAREDNESS AND SELF-RELIANCE

The only aspect of disasters that is predictable is that they are unpredictable. With very few exceptions, disasters have the reputation of catching you off guard and striking when you least expect. Over the last few decades, disasters have changed the world in ways we could have never imagined. Looking back, there was always one common theme: These disasters had profound impacts on unprepared communities versus those who were prepared.

The impact of being unprepared, either mentally or physically, can be severe. Not only is there a risk of personal injury and death, but you can also lose your home, personal belongings, job, business, savings, and even entire community. A sudden and unexpected disaster can rob your stability, security, sense of normalcy, and even dignity. Everything you love and have worked for can disappear in one fell swoop.

Preparedness leads down a path of deeper self-reliance. Self-reliance is the idea of being able to provide for oneself and not relying on the powers or resources of other people or a government. This should not be confused, however, with establishing a network and community of trusted people with whom to share support and resources. More on the importance of community and network development will be discussed in detail later. When we think of being prepared for disaster, self-reliance is the goal, even if for a short period of time. In this chapter, you will learn the benefits of preparedness both physically and mentally and how being prepared can increase your self-reliance and chances of survival.

The Role of Preparedness in Mitigating Risks

While no level of preparedness can eliminate all risk associated with any given disaster, there is no doubt that preparedness efforts can help mitigate some risk. And, as has been proven time and time again, being prepared can make the difference between life and death. Sheer survival aside, there are countless other benefits to being prepared. Subscribing to the belief that "disaster only happens to other people" can have devastating consequences.

Fireproofing is a great example. For those who live in the wildfire zones of California, strategies such as replacing your roof with noncombustible materials, eliminating gaps in attic vents to prevent embers from getting inside, removing flammable vegetation from around the home, and cleaning debris from gutters can lessen the effects of a forest fire on and around the home. In many cases, these tactics can completely prevent a fire from spreading to the home altogether, and maybe even throughout an entire neighborhood.

For people who work in large office buildings, preparing an escape and evacuation plan in advance can prevent mass panic and keep people from being unnecessarily trapped in the event that a disaster leads to evacuation.

On a more basic level, water storage can prevent people from dying of thirst. Food storage can prevent starvation. A two-week backstock of critical medication can prevent death from chronic illness. The list of good reasons to prepare goes on and on.

Being Psychologically Prepared

Physical loss is only one aspect to consider. Disasters and their effects can cause fear, anxiety, and post-traumatic stress disorder, especially in children. I can think of no better reason to be prepared than to lessen the emotional impact of disaster. Not only does having a plan reduce anxiety before a disaster, but it will reduce stress during one as well.

It is easy for people to fall into a trap of helplessness either before or during a disaster. This trap often prevents them from doing anything constructive, whether it's preparing in advance or taking proper steps. While it's true that no one can control a disaster, it is not true that you have no control at all. The actions you take before and during a disaster absolutely have an effect on the outcome for you and your loved ones. Controlling and managing emotions can help eliminate any counterproductive feelings of helplessness and replace them with purpose and a desire for self-reliance. Try using the following strategies to control and manage emotions:

A.I.M.

The Australian Psychological Society prescribes "Anticipate," "Identify," and "Manage" for psychological preparedness, which I have simplified into a memorable acronym that can be used to help you be psychologically prepared: A.I.M.

A—Anticipate
I—Identify
M—Manage

Let's discuss why each of these is important.

Anticipate

Trying to anticipate how you will feel when disaster strikes can be a useful strategy for managing and controlling your emotions during the actual disaster. Expecting a high level of stress can prepare you to react appropriately to that stress. Managing expectations is very effective in managing stress.

Identify

Stress and fear manifest in physical reactions such as nausea, shaking, panic, and a racing heart. These physical symptoms then worsen feelings of stress and fear, and it becomes a vicious cycle that only makes any situation worse. Understanding and identifying how you physically react to anxiety can help you better control your emotional reactions while under the stress of a disaster.

Manage

Managing your responses to emotional stress during a disaster is critical. Controlling your breathing and focusing on executing your preparedness plan are both tactics that can help.

COMBAT BREATHING

There is a very effective breathing tactic used by the military and first responders to help manage stress when under extreme pressure, called combat breathing. Here's how to do it:

1. Start by breathing in while counting 1, 2, 3, 4.
2. Then, stop and hold your breath while counting 1, 2, 3, 4.
3. Finally, exhale while counting 1, 2, 3, 4.

This series of controlled and focused breaths is then repeated until the desired result is achieved. A breathing exercise may sound like a waste of time, but controlling your reaction to extreme stress and regaining focus is a lifesaving skill in the midst of chaos.

Self-Reliance in Emergencies

In a disaster, the first person you can rely on is yourself. Self-reliant individuals, versus those who are dependent on the resources of others, are better positioned to handle emergencies. Self-reliance is the ability to act on one's own and to achieve certain goals without the help of someone else. Self-reliance requires planning, preparation, and an investment of time and resources. It also requires confidence, action, skills, and perseverance.

Self-reliance isn't just about providing physical things such as food, water, electricity, shelter, and tools. It equally is reliance on one's internal resources. Simply put, it is not enough to have "stuff." The mentality of self-reliance is critical. The good news is that wherever you are on the scale of self-reliance right now, both physically and mentally, it is possible to become more self-reliant.

The Self-Reliant Mindset

A self-reliant-minded person is first and foremost a sharp problem-solver. The ability to pivot and solve one's own problems is one of the most important skills to have in any survival or disaster scenario. It is said that people who grew up fast develop this skill set early on out of necessity. Those who are coddled or taken care of by others have an undeveloped problem-solving skill set. Luckily, just like with any other skill, problem-solving gets easier with practice. Here are some qualities of self-reliant people:

- **Self-reliant people also understand the value of self-care.** If your "self" isn't well and ready to face a challenge, then your ability to be truly self-reliant suffers. Lack of self-care results in increased anxiety, increased stress, decreased motivation, chronic illness, and poor physical fitness.
- **Self-reliant people can also handle pressure and responsibility.** As the saying goes, "When the going gets tough, the tough get going." You can measure the self-reliance of an individual by the number of excuses they give when faced with adversity. Do they complain, or dig in and act? Think about the people in your life you would call on when things get hard. These people are likely self-reliant.
- **Self-reliant people also empower and help others to be self-reliant.** Their "never give up" attitude is motivating and encouraging. If your goal is to be more self-reliant, identify the self-reliant people in your life and spend more time with them. Humans tend to become like people they spend time with. Self-reliant traits are contagious.

Self-Reliant Skill Sets

As important as mindset is in a disaster scenario, one must also have a set of skills. A self-reliant-minded person has both. While there are countless valuable disaster survival skill sets, some are absolute necessities. These include but are not limited to:

- Basic first aid and trauma skills
- Food preservation, storage, and preparation skills
- Water purification, treatment, and sourcing skills
- Radio communication skills

These skill sets all help meet basic human survival needs, and this guide will cover each of them and more in detail in later chapters. For each skill set you lack, your dependence on others increases. Any level of dependency opens potential pitfalls.

Bridging the gap between dependency and self-reliance requires an honest and thorough personal risk assessment. Understanding one's vulnerabilities is not only a key aspect of self-reliance but also the first step in putting together a disaster-ready plan.

CHAPTER 2

RISK ASSESSMENT AND PERSONAL VULNERABILITIES

It is human nature to believe that disasters only happen to other people or in other geographic areas. When disasters strike, they always seem to be a complete surprise even though disasters of all shapes, sizes, and causes are happening every day on some part of the globe. If you have not already, it is time to come to grips with the notion that it's not *IF* but *WHEN* some kind of disaster will strike and affect life as you know it. Once you realize this, the next step is to begin a thorough risk assessment. This process can help identify risks and vulnerabilities and provide an actionable foundation for putting together a preparedness plan that makes sense.

Risk Assessment

Simply put, a risk assessment is a process used to identify potential dangers with the intent of predicting and analyzing what could happen. Because there is more than one potential disaster, it is common to do multiple risk assessments. A risk assessment is essentially a process of gathering knowledge that can be used to create an actionable plan. Without a risk assessment that sheds light on the disaster itself, your level of exposure, your vulnerabilities, and your potential losses (physical, property, financial, emotional), any readiness plan is incomplete.

CONDUCTING A PERSONAL/FAMILY RISK ASSESSMENT

There are countless different versions of a personal disaster risk assessment. But any solid risk assessment includes at minimum the following basic considerations:

- **Risk Identification:** This includes identifying any potential hazards/ disasters.
- **Exposure Analysis and Vulnerability Evaluation:** This step involves deciding who or what might be harmed by the potential risks. In addition, an effort should be made to determine the level of potential impact to each vulnerability.
- **Risk Reduction:** This stage involves identifying specific precautions that need to be taken to prevent, lessen, or mitigate damage to the vulnerabilities listed in the previous step.
- **Preparedness Plan:** Lastly, using the information gathered in the previous steps, it's time to outline a formal Personal/Family Preparedness Plan and start acting.

Now that you have a thousand-foot view of a personal risk assessment, it's time to break down each of the sections into more detailed actionable steps.

Risk Identification

The first step is to identify the disasters that are most likely to happen. Different areas of the world are prone to different disasters. If you live in Kansas, tornadoes should be at the top of your list. If you live in New Orleans, hurricanes should take the top spot. Residents of New York City may list a grid-down power outage as a potential disaster. History is a good teacher and often repeats itself. Risk identification is unique to you, your community, and your location.

The main goal of this step is to identify any possible hazard that may potentially cause harm to you, your home, your business, your family, your school, or anything else you value. Preparedness starts with thinking about the possibilities.

This is a great time to get your family involved. Even better would be to get your neighbors involved in the conversation. Then, collectively brainstorm what types of disasters have happened before in your area and what types are most likely to happen. You may be surprised at the list that comes out of this session. It will certainly include hazards you may have never considered. Furthermore, ask your local municipality to share their existing community emergency plans. It is likely that numerous sectors have weighed in on these plans. These could include firefighters, corporate emergency managers, engineers, government officials, geologists, floodplain managers, law enforcement, and other community groups. These resources can provide fresh and unique insights into what you should be planning for on a personal or family level. If your community doesn't have an emergency manager or official plans in place, look to the next closest large community. Community emergency managers are often friendly and eager to share their knowledge.

The state where you live already has detailed documentation about potential hazards that may affect your community. To locate the emergency management website for your state, visit USA.gov/state-emergency-management. You may find that much of the work has already been done for you when it comes to brainstorming potential hazards.

In addition to your state's online emergency management resources, become familiar with these common hazard data sources. Your tax dollars fund them.

- **US Department of Homeland Security—Ready.gov.** The Department of Homeland Security's Ready.gov is a public service that provides education related to preparation and response to natural and man-made disasters. This website not only provides information on preparedness but also outlines many different types of hazards.
- **Federal Emergency Management Agency (FEMA).** FEMA provides information related to identifying hazards and preparing a risk assessment: FEMA.gov/hazard-mitigation-planning-resources.
- **National Centers for Environmental Information.** This is a great online data source for weather information. It keeps historical data on a wide variety of storm events: NCDC.NOAA.gov/stormevents.

- **National Weather Service (NWS).** The NWS is the official provider of US weather, marine, fire, and aviation forecasts. It is an agency of the National Oceanic and Atmospheric Administration (NOAA) and lists a glossary of over two thousand phrases and terms used by the NWS: Forecast.Weather.gov/glossary.php.
- **United States Geological Survey (USGS).** If you live in an area where earthquakes or landslides are on the radar, the USGS is a resource you'll want to visit. It hosts data pertaining to landslide and earthquake hazards: USGS.gov/natural_hazards.

Once a final list of disasters is created, it's time to rank these threats. You should rank them in order of probability, with the most probable disaster ranking first. Next, you'll analyze what areas of your life are most vulnerable to these threats and how serious is the potential harm.

Exposure Analysis and Vulnerability Evaluation

Once hazards are identified, it's time to do two things: analyze exposure and evaluate vulnerability. This is essentially making a list of who or what might be harmed and how badly. This process will help you gauge how serious the previously established risks are to the assets in your life and will aid in prioritizing actions later. The terms *exposure* and *vulnerability* are often misunderstood. Simply put, *exposure* refers to people, property, buildings, finances, and even emotions. These are the things you care about that could be harmed by a disaster. *Vulnerability* is the likelihood that these exposures will be harmed or affected negatively by the disaster.

To start, it's important to create your list of exposures. To help with this phase, I've created a simple downloadable worksheet you can use. You can find the Exposure and Vulnerability Worksheet at the online resource link for this book: CreekStewart.com/disasterready. As mentioned, exposures are the things you care about. Look at it this way: If something was negatively affected by the disaster, would you miss it? If the answer is yes, it's an exposure. For Personal/Family Preparedness Plans, most exposures will fall into three main categories:

physical, social, and economic. Examples might include people, finances, structures, businesses, personal property, land, inventory, and more. Make a list or fill in the worksheet with as many exposures as you can think of. For reference, here is a short list with examples of how disaster can affect the three areas:

Physical
- Structural damage
- Access to structures
- Property loss/damage
- Vehicle damage

Social
- Death
- Injury
- Emotional damage
- Loss of pets

Economic
- Loss of business
- Interruption of business
- Loss of employment
- Loss of financial assets
- Loss of employees

Next, you should evaluate how vulnerable the important exposures (people and things) previously identified are to each disaster risk you identified earlier. Ultimately, you'll have a dedicated worksheet for each disaster. There are many ways to measure vulnerability, and some of them can get quite complicated. I recommend keeping it simple with a 0–10 rating, 0 meaning the exposure is not vulnerable (not likely to be affected) and 10 meaning the exposure is at a very high risk of being harmed.

Many factors influence vulnerability. Some are obvious and some aren't. Following is a list of factors to consider when rating vulnerability for several common exposures. There are several blank spaces for you to fill in, in case I've missed factors that are personal to you.

Exposure: Physical

- Age of structure
- Construction style
- Existing structural issues or weaknesses
- Location of property or structures (e.g., in a floodplain)
- Applicable insurance policies
- Inherent threats located nearby (e.g., a nuclear power plant)

- _____
- _____
- _____

Exposure: Social

- Age (being young or an older person increases vulnerability)
- Physical fitness
- Handicaps/disabilities
- Medical conditions
- Gender
- Income
- Location (living in a high-density area such as New York City increases vulnerability)
- Dependency on medicine

- _____
- _____
- _____

Exposure: Economic

- Is a disaster emergency fund in place?
- Are disaster supplies in place (e.g., food storage, water storage)?
- Is yours a one- or two-income family?
- Are additional income sources available?
- Are savings assets at risk?
- Is job loss a risk?
- What if transportation is interrupted and a commute isn't possible?

- _____

- _____

- _____

Once you complete the Exposure and Vulnerability Worksheet for each of your top disaster threats, you'll have a picture of what exposures (people and things) are most vulnerable. Thus begins the process of addressing vulnerabilities. The entire purpose of this exercise is to help you quickly and effectively identify holes in your preparedness plan that need to be dealt with. We call these holes needs.

My friend Nat Sellers is a professional emergency manager and has a master's degree in emergency and disaster management. Nat has created a fantastic Hazards Assessment Worksheet that helps outline and organize your needs and priorities in this process. He has given me permission to offer this worksheet to you as a free download and you can find it at the online resource page for this book: CreekStewart.com/disasterready. Nat also has some excellent resources at his website, PreparednessGuy.com.

This process takes you from the thousand-foot view to a specific list of needs that should be addressed for each and every disaster at the top of your list. With an idea of vulnerabilities, you'll be able to quickly complete a needs assessment for categories such as food, water, cooking, housing, power, and more. The Exposure and Vulnerability Worksheet will help you break down your most important needs into immediate, short-term, mid-term, and long-term needs. Take some time to download and complete this worksheet.

Risk Reduction

The combination of awareness and actions of preparedness will result in risk reduction. Without getting too complicated, the more you understand your vulnerabilities and the more action steps you take to resolve them, the less overall risk you will have. Limited risk is an overarching goal of preparedness.

There's no doubt that this process can take some time. But I've learned, through years of teaching and practicing these lessons, that the more knowledge you can gather up front, the better you can plan. I'll be digging into many of the top needs categories in detail later. But before we do that, I want to share an outline for a solid Personal/Family Preparedness Plan. This is the absolute bare minimum that every family should have in place. It includes essential information to know and steps to take that are critical in the event of a sudden and unexpected emergency.

Personal/Family Preparedness Plan

A Personal/Family Preparedness Plan is a set of documents in place that everyone in your household is familiar with and knows where to access in the event of an emergency. Ideally this plan is kept as a PDF on family devices such as phones and tablets. Physical copies can be posted on the refrigerator or another easy-to-remember spot in the home. This document set is essentially your road map for what everyone in your family does in the event of an emergency. It takes the guesswork out of many critical decisions and actions and makes decisions easier and quicker.

It is very unlikely that everyone will be together in the same spot when disaster strikes. A Personal/Family Preparedness Plan helps mitigate the inevitable chaos and prevent unnecessary stress and mistakes. Some of these steps may seem basic and obvious, but make sure to complete all of them.

PART 1: FAMILY COMMUNICATIONS PLAN

A Family Communications Plan is an outline of directives and information for how to get in touch with each other if you're at work, school, or away from the home. It also contains a list of important contacts with phone numbers. This information helps family members communicate if normal methods of communication aren't working. Refer to Chapter 8 for a full outline of a Family Communications Plan.

PART 2: EVACUATION PLAN

Many disasters force people to leave their homes. It's important to have a plan in place for safely and efficiently evacuating your family if this happens. Every evacuation plan should include the following elements:

- Make sure everyone knows where to locate your 72-hour emergency kit (bug out bag). This kit will include everything you need for independent survival during an evacuation: tools, food, water, first aid, hygiene items, and more. (Details of building this kit will be covered in Chapter 13.) Don't forget supplies for your pets.
- Establish three evacuation destinations outside your general area. One should be 1–2 hours away, one should be 3–5 hours away, and one should be several states away. These can be a relative's or friend's house. Have paper maps to each of these locations for you and your family members to use.
- Review all possible exits from the home during an emergency. For two-story homes, include the use of emergency window ladders.
- Map all possible routes to your in-town and out-of-town evacuation destinations.
- Always try to keep at least a half tank of gas in the car. Consider keeping a couple of containers of gas at home as a backup supply. You can use an additive called STA-BIL to keep the gas good for long periods of time. Gas stations will be clogged during evacuations.
- Consider a backup method of transportation such as an electric bicycle (more on this topic in Chapter 14).
- Turn off all utilities including gas, water, and electricity. Drain water pipes if you have time, especially in cold weather.
- Lock all doors, windows, and entrances to the home. Utilize the home security tips offered in Chapter 10.

PART 3: EMERGENCY SKILLS TO KNOW AND PRACTICE

While not an exhaustive list, here are some key emergency skills that each capable member of your family should know and practice. The time to familiarize oneself with these is before a disaster strikes.

- Make sure every family member knows where the fire extinguishers are in the house and how to use them.
- Be sure every household member knows where and how to shut off the following utilities: water, gas, electricity.
- Understand how to use all electronics including handheld radios and NOAA-capable radios (detailed in Chapter 8).
- Make sure everyone is trained in basic first aid and CPR (cardiopulmonary resuscitation).

PART 4: BASIC CHECKLIST OF THINGS TO DO

Following is a checklist of several key actions to take to become better prepared for virtually any disaster scenario. By the end of this book you should be able to confidently check each of these off the list.

- Obtain homeowners insurance and add additional coverage for disasters on your priority list that aren't covered under your policy.
- Get your family a General Mobile Radio Service (GMRS) license (detailed in Chapter 8).
- Build a 72-hour emergency kit or bug out bag (detailed in Chapter 13).
- Prepare your home to shelter in place for an extended period in case you have to "hunker down." (Details will be covered in subsequent chapters.)

Getting a Personal/Family Preparedness Plan on paper takes work and becomes a foundation to build upon. Almost everything discussed up to this point has been focused on you and your family. However, one of the biggest underestimated and overlooked resources in disaster preparedness is your immediate neighbors and community. There is power, safety, resilience, and wisdom in numbers. The next chapter will discuss how your community and neighbors can be one of the most powerful assets you can have in a disaster scenario.

PART 2

STAY

Ultimately, disasters will present you with two options: Stay or Go. You must be prepared to make that decision at a moment's notice. Making this decision requires not only the knowledge to assess the situation properly but also the physical tools, gear, and preps to back up that decision with action.

In this part of the book, we will address the decision to stay, aka shelter in place. Some circumstances require you to hunker down in your home and weather the storm. This may be because it is safer to do so or because there is some reason you cannot evacuate. Regardless, sheltering in place means that you may need to provide for yourself and your family without the usual access to electricity, food, water, heating options, and more. Disasters often disrupt what is considered normal when it comes to meeting basic human survival needs and require you to operate in a more self-sufficient way for an undetermined period of time.

The following chapters will outline strategies for you to pro-vide yourself and your family with food, water, heat, communica-tions, off-grid power, first aid, self-defense, and more. Depending on your risk assessment and personal vulnerabilities, you may choose to focus on one, some, or all of the preparedness categories discussed. For each category, you'll discover actionable steps so that you can become more confident, capable, and self-sufficient in the event you need to shelter in place.

CHAPTER 3

NETWORK DEVELOPMENT

It takes a village to face a disaster. While "going it alone" may seem to have appeal in the movies, it is a very poor strategy in the real world. The truth is that there is great power and resilience in numbers. Nurturing a small network of trusted friends and neighbors can be one of the most important disaster-related strategies you will implement. This chapter will not only highlight why a survival network is critical to your disaster preparedness plan but will also outline some ideas to help you develop one.

The Power of Relationships in Disasters

Contrary to what many might think, local, state, and federal governments aren't the heroes during a disaster crisis. We've learned all too well that these responses are typically slow and bound with red tape. Money doesn't solve problems in disaster; relationships do. In addition, first responders are overwhelmed during a large-scale crisis, and response times are slow, unpredictable, and sometimes nonexistent.

In 2011, National Public Radio ran a piece titled "The Key to Disaster Survival? Friends and Neighbors." It was a spot-on discussion of what really matters during disaster. Communities are made up of neighborhoods, streets, and cul-de-sacs. Each of these comprise homes filled with people who have varying skill sets, supplies, resources, and needs. These neighbors are the first line of help during crisis. As was seen during the Hurricane Katrina disaster, where it took federal officials several weeks to reach some communities, neighbors were crucial to survival. Your immediate help during and after a disaster will not come from local, state, or federal governments; it will come from your neighbors. And the street travels both ways.

A solid neighborhood disaster preparedness plan is composed of six elements:

1. Knowing and Mapping Your Neighborhood
2. Creating a Tiered Neighborhood Communications Plan
3. Identifying Neighborhood Risks
4. Identifying Neighborhood Skills
5. Identifying Neighborhood Resources
6. Developing a Neighborhood Security Plan

The city of Austin, Texas, has an existing worksheet that you can print out to help organize the information in the first five categories. I suggest printing out the last several pages of this worksheet and using them as you review each of the six elements. You can find those pages under the Chapter 3 heading at the online resource page for this book: CreekStewart.com/disasterready.

Hosting a Neighborhood Preparedness Meeting

As you review the six elements of a neighborhood disaster preparedness plan, think about them in the context of hosting a neighborhood preparedness meeting. This is simply a gathering of neighbors to discuss a plan in advance of a potential disaster. All six elements are great topics to discuss in a meeting with neighbors. Such a discussion gets everyone involved and is a good opportunity to identify who has greater needs or risks, who has what skills, and who may be willing to share certain resources in the event of a disaster. Any true neighborhood preparedness plan will require at least one meeting a year to discuss and update information.

These neighborhood meetings are also a great way to get to know your neighbors if you don't already. Remember, research shows that the people who know the most people are the ones that fare best in a disaster scenario.

Having hosted meetings like these and having worked with dozens of others who have as well, I can tell you that you'll get a much higher turnout if you personally invite your neighbors to the meeting. It's easier to email or drop off a flyer, but a face-to-face invitation goes a long way when inviting someone to a preparedness meeting.

If you want to host a neighborhood preparedness meeting, the Washington State Emergency Management Division has put together a great guide that is worth reviewing to help outline such a meeting. For your convenience, I've made the guide available to you at the online resource page for this book: CreekStewart.com/disasterready.

Knowing and Mapping Your Neighborhood

You'd be surprised how many people don't know their neighbors just a few doors down the street. If you live in a neighborhood or in the suburbs, your neighborhood map should include at least the nearest twenty-five neighbors. If you live in a rural area where homes are more spread out, it will likely include fewer.

A neighborhood map is simply a hand-drawn or computer-generated map of your immediate neighbors who may be your allies in a disaster. It may be helpful to reference *Google Earth* to help draw the map. This will give you a bird's-eye view of your area. Your neighborhood map should clearly show streets and each of the homes on them. Full names of residents, house numbers, and phone numbers should be listed with each home on the map so that this information is quickly available. It is also a good idea to clearly mark any specific neighborhood meeting places in the event of a neighborhood-wide disaster.

If you're hosting a neighborhood preparedness meeting, these maps make great handouts to get the discussion started about who lives where and help in completing the contact information if data is missing.

Creating a Tiered Neighborhood Communications Plan

When I was a kid, my mom was a vice principal of a local high school. Whenever her school was canceled due to snow, she would get a call from the principal. Then, she would be responsible for calling four teachers, who were then responsible for calling four more teachers each. In just a few minutes, this tiered communications approach would alert all staff at the school that it was closed for the day. Today, a group text thread can be even more effective for communicating critical information to all neighbors. But if for some reason it's important to communicate via phone instead, it's a good idea to have a tiered neighborhood phone plan in place. This is especially true if you have older neighbors who may not use text messaging. Microsoft PowerPoint has a feature called SmartArt that makes creating a tiered list very easy. Consider making one and distributing copies to all your neighbors who wish to participate. Following is a graphic illustration as a sample for you to follow.

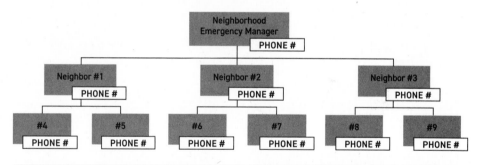

Distribute copies of a neighborhood phone plan like this one to all your neighbors who wish to participate.

In addition to a tiered phone list, it is important that each neighbor complete a communications form that includes the following information:

- Adult name(s)
- Children name(s)
- Best phone number
- Email address

- Pets (name and kind)
- Family member(s) with special needs

These forms can be compiled in a binder that can be referenced in the event of a neighborhood-wide event.

Identifying Neighborhood Risks

Identifying neighborhood risks starts the same way as devising your Personal/Family Preparedness Plan: by identifying disaster risks specific to your neighborhood. If you've already made a preparedness plan, these risks will likely be the same. Understanding such risks is important to help put the remaining three elements in context.

In addition to a listing of disasters, it's important to identify neighbors with specific needs such as people with disabilities, older people, or families with small children. History has proved these groups to be more vulnerable to disaster, and knowing who and where they live helps less vulnerable neighbors check on them quickly and efficiently. Having each neighbor complete a communications form can provide this information.

Identifying Neighborhood Skills

Knowing the skill sets of your neighbors is critical to quick and efficient disaster recovery. An organized skills list can provide information for whom to call if the need arises.

Many skills are needed during and after a crisis. These can include but are not limited to first aid, construction, disaster preparedness, childcare, ham radio operation, senior care, pet care, and trade skills such as plumbing and electricity. Everyone likely has some kind of skill that can be deployed in the event of a disaster. Even someone with a physical impairment can be a communications manager. Knowing who possesses what skills can save precious time in the chaos of a disaster. Ask each neighbor to list any skills they'd be willing to volunteer in the event of a crisis.

Identifying Neighborhood Resources

Neighborhood resources are physical resources that neighbors would be willing to offer for use during a crisis. Examples might be a chainsaw, shovel and tools, boat, tractor, small excavator, extra lumber, extra generator, handheld radios, spare cots, and more. Each home will have different resources, and this allows everyone to contribute in a meaningful way.

Again, a list of these physical resources can be kept in a binder so that individuals can be quickly contacted if that particular resource is needed and available for use. This process may also identify gaps in the plan that you or someone else may want to consider filling.

Developing a Neighborhood Security Plan

It's no secret that crime spikes under the cloak and chaos of disaster (Chapter 10 will cover self and home defense in detail). For this reason, your neighborhood may consider putting together a formal neighborhood security plan. This plan can be as simple as neighbors keeping an extra-watchful eye to a full 24/7 neighborhood security detail. Here are several items to consider when developing a neighborhood security plan:

- Establish a tiered communication plan and neighborhood text thread as detailed previously. This can help communicate threats throughout the neighborhood quickly and efficiently.
- Encourage homes to install a security system.
- Encourage neighbors to post security system signs in their yards. The more homes with these, the better.
- Encourage neighbors to install motion sensor lights. Nighttime lighting is one of the best crime deterrents there is.
- Keep yards clean and tidy. Criminals love big bushes and other places to hide.
- Consider installing solar street lighting if your neighborhood is dark and hard to navigate at night.

- Encourage neighbors to text the network if they see something out of place. It's better to be safe than sorry.
- Establish off-grid means of neighborhood communication (discussed in Chapter 8) such as handheld radios. Be sure that all neighbors who wish to participate purchase the same radio and know the neighborhood security channel. This is critical if cell phone service is interrupted.
- Consider holding a meeting about home hardening. Invite local police to the meeting to present ways to harden your home against unauthorized entry, such as sturdier doors, deadbolts, bigger hinges, and even a watch-dog. Chapter 10 provides many ideas as well.
- Compile a list of security volunteers who may consider conducting neighborhood patrols if there are repeated signs of odd activity during a crisis. Always patrol in pairs or more.

For more information about establishing a Neighborhood Watch program and for other checklist resources available to help with neighborhood security, consider visiting the National Crime Prevention Council at NCPC.org/resources/home-neighborhood-safety/#.

As well-intended as you may be in engaging neighbors to be involved in a neighborhood plan, not everyone will be interested. The reasons for this vary and include apathy, shame for their own lack of preparedness or resources, a feeling of nothing to offer in this area, or a desire to be private and left alone. All of these are valid reasons and should be respected.

However, I've found there is a way to bridge the gap created by many of these reasons: free training that everyone can learn from. Holding a free how-to training for your neighbors is a great way not only to get the conversation started about preparedness but also to get to know them as well. One of the best training courses for this purpose is how to prepare some basic food items for long-term storage. It seems almost everyone is interested in this topic these days. The following chapter will discuss not only the importance of having a disaster food storage plan but also several different strategies for safely storing food long term.

CHAPTER 4

FOOD STORAGE AND MANAGEMENT

There is a saying within the disaster preparedness community: America is nine meals away from anarchy. One could likely name many countries in place of America in that saying. What this means is that most homes only have nine meals' worth of food on hand at any given moment. If the food supply chain becomes interrupted, most communities are nine meals away from having some serious problems.

While food isn't our most important human survival need, it is at the epicenter of preparedness. Most people's very definition of survival is tied directly to hunger. Having trained with thousands of people over the past two decades, I've learned that the vast majority of people fear being hungry more than anything else.

This chapter will discuss not only the basics of disaster food storage but also the types of food to store and how to store them. I'll also be teaching you some proven methods for storing food for very long periods of time if your preparedness goals are beyond three to six months.

Basics of Food Storage

Before we delve into the types and methods of food storage, let's first discuss some fundamental principles that you must understand about selection, shelf life, and storage conditions. If you miss these, all your efforts could be thwarted.

There are five things that will ruin, compromise, or cause your food to have a shorter shelf life. They are humidity, air (oxygen), temperature, sunlight, and pests. Each must be considered when building a long-term storage pantry.

MOISTURE

Moisture will ruin food quicker than almost anything else. If food draws in moisture, it can cause mold and bacteria to grow. Moisture can also compromise packaging, especially paper packaging and metal cans. For this reason, all food storage should be kept inside a protected and temperature-controlled room inside your home. If the room has moisture, such as a basement, consider purchasing a dehumidifier. When storing goods long term, it's important to trade out any paper or cardboard packaging for waterproof alternatives such as plastic buckets. I'll discuss exactly how to do this later in the chapter.

AIR (OXYGEN)

A study in the *Journal of Food Science and Technology* best describes the effects of oxygen on longer-term food storage:

> The various effects of oxygen on preserved foods and beverages includes rancidity of unsaturated fats (i.e., 'off-flavors' and toxic end-products), darkening of fresh meat pigments by promoting the growth of aerobic bacteria and fungi, stale odour of soft bakery foods and phenolic browning of fruit/vegetables.

When oxygen is reduced, the environment improves when it comes to food preservation and shelf life. This is why you'll often find oxygen-absorbing packets inside many packaged food products you buy at the grocery store. Later in the chapter, we'll discuss how to include oxygen-absorbing packets when you put up food for long-term storage.

TEMPERATURE

A study at Brigham Young University showed that dry wheat berries stored perfectly well for twenty-five years when kept in a cool, dry basement but only lasted five years when stored in a hot garage or attic. Heat is an enemy to food storage.

SUNLIGHT

If you've ever left anything on your car dashboard, then you already know the detrimental effects of sunlight. Sunlight not only raises temperature, but it also breaks down packaging and degrades food quality. Never store food in direct sunlight. If your storage room has a window, be sure to block any direct sunlight with thick blinds or curtains.

PESTS

A friend told me once that he opened a bucket of oatmeal he had stored for several years, and he thought his eyes were playing tricks on him. The oatmeal was moving! But it wasn't his eyes; the container was filled with weevil larvae. Yuck!

Pests include rodents and insects primarily. Measures should be taken to keep both at bay. These measures should include using durable packaging, storing food off the ground on wire racks, setting traps in and around the storage area, and keeping the storage area clean. Oxygen absorbers added to food storage can help create an environment incompatible with life for many insects. Freezing dry goods for two weeks can kill insect eggs that may hatch later. Also, adding diatomaceous earth to dry goods stored long term will kill many insects if they hatch. (More on this will be discussed later in the chapter.)

Types of Foods for Long-Term Storage

When it comes to emergency food storage, my suggestion is to keep it very simple. The simplest kind of emergency food storage meets the following criteria:

- Does not require gas or electricity to store.
- Has a shelf life of at least one year.

- Is food you eat on a regular basis (at least for the first three months of storage).
- Is simple to prepare.

These criteria obviously eliminate many foods, including fresh vegetables, meats, and any perishable items in the refrigerator or freezer. These will be the first foods to spoil after a disaster and aren't reliable for long-term storage. While I agree that these are the healthiest foods, they do not make the best options for long-term storage.

Following is a list of foods that make excellent candidates for mid- to long-term storage using the three methods of food storage I outline next in the chapter. You'll find these foods mainly in the inner isles of a grocery store:

- Canned tuna, salmon, chicken, or turkey (with shelf life of at least one year)
- Canned vegetables, such as green beans, carrots, and peas (with shelf life of at least one year)
- Canned soups and chili (with shelf life of at least one year)
- Dry boxed goods and mixes (with shelf life of at least one year)
- Dry pastas
- Dry rice
- Dry beans
- Cereals
- Oats
- Peanut butter (with shelf life of at least one year)
- Nuts and trail mixes (with shelf life of at least one year)

These categories cover a lot of different food options. The canned goods alone represent an endless variety of options.

Food Preservation

There are dozens of food preservation options ranging from dehydration and wet canning to salting and smoking. You could spend days researching which methods are best and most practical for long-term storage. I'm going to make this really simple for you and detail what I believe are the three most practical methods to focus on when it comes to building your long-term storage pantry:

- **Rotation:** A process of building and rotating the stock of food you already eat on a regular basis.
- **Freeze-Dried Food:** Includes purchasing freeze-dried meals that can be reconstituted with water or freeze-drying your own meals at home.
- **Long-Term Storage of Bulk Dry Goods:** A process of purchasing bulk dry goods such as beans and rice and repackaging them at home so that they will last twenty-five-plus years in storage.

You'll notice that I don't include at-home canning in this list. While at-home canning is an excellent long-term food storage method, I do not believe it is the most practical for most people these days, especially those who do not grow their own fruits and vegetables. For this reason, I have left it out. In the following sections, I detail each method for you to choose which one (or combination) best fits your lifestyle, budget, and diet.

METHOD 1: ROTATION

Time period: Up to one year

There is a saying that I love: Store what you eat and eat what you store. This simple saying is at the heart of the rotation storage philosophy. Rotation is the process of slowly building up a backstock of the top ten to twenty-five shelf-stable foods you and your family eat most often. After making a list of these most frequently eaten foods, a backstock can be built over time by purchasing a few extras of each item on regular grocery trips and as your budget allows. These items are kept in a spare room or closet, and as you use up the food in your kitchen pantry, you rotate the stock from your backup storage to ensure that no food items expire. As long as you're constantly rotating through your backstock food and purchasing more, you'll always have food that is not expired. I know people who have one year's worth of food stored in a cycle of rotation, but this isn't practical for most people. Rotation works well for people who want to store up to three months' worth of food. It is worth noting that using this storage option is a lifestyle decision. This integrates storage into your regular routine of shopping, cooking, and eating.

METHOD 2: FREEZE-DRIED FOOD

Time period: Twenty-five-plus years

Freeze-dried food is the perfect set-it-and-forget-it disaster food storage option. Freeze-drying is *a form of dehydration*. Fresh food is first frozen, then dried under pressure to remove its water content. It's an incredible process that has countless benefits over other preservation methods. Some of these include:

- Has a shelf-life of twenty-five-plus years.
- Maintains 97 percent of nutritional value versus 60 percent in dehydrated food and 40 percent in canned food.
- Maintains color and texture.
- Only requires water to reconstitute.

If you've ever eaten a camping meal where you had to add boiling water to the foil pouch, then you've had a freeze-dried meal. These meals are very popular among campers and hikers because they are very lightweight and simple to prepare. Space ice cream is also a freeze-dried product. According to Harvest Right, a manufacturer of at-home freeze-drying machines, almost any food product can be freeze-dried, including fruits, vegetables, meats, desserts, dairy, and entire meals. Items that aren't good freeze-dry candidates are mainly oily foods such as peanut butter, pure chocolate, butter, honey, syrup, and jam. Many freeze-dried foods make excellent hiking and road trip snacks even without rehydration. These include fruits such as blueberries and bananas and even broccoli florets.

The versatility and convenience of freeze-dried food comes at a premium. It is the most expensive of all long-term food storage options.

Freeze-dried food maintains 97 percent of the food's nutritional value over twenty-five-plus years.

Prepackaged buckets of freeze-dried chicken, milk, eggs, vegetables, and fruits aren't cheap. You could easily spend thousands of dollars on a few months' supply for your family. Even if you're on a tight budget, I would encourage you to build up a two-week supply of freeze-dried meals for your family in case of emergency. If disaster strikes, freeze-dried meals are very easy to prepare and very nutritious. Having these meals on hand can solve a big problem while you focus your energy on other concerns such as heat, construction, first aid, and other necessities.

There are many different manufacturers and retailers of freeze-dried food products. Some of my favorite brands are ReadyWise and Peak Refuel. For your convenience, I have created a short list with web links at the online resource page for this book: CreekStewart.com/disasterready.

For about $2,500 you can purchase an at-home freeze-drying machine from Harvest Right. This machine will allow you to produce your own freeze-dried food storage at home for a fraction of the price it would cost you to buy the food from a retailer. Harvest Right estimates that freeze-drying your own food costs one-third the amount of buying the food from a store. If you like the idea of freeze-dried food and have a do-it-yourself personality, this could very well be the best option for you and your family. I have a friend who paid for his freeze-dry machine by selling freeze-dried candy at local farmers markets. Brilliant! For the freeze-dry machine I recommend, visit the online resource page for this book: CreekStewart.com/disasterready.

METHOD 3: LONG-TERM STORAGE OF BULK DRY GOODS

Time period: Twenty-five-plus years

For the budget-conscious consumer who also wants to build a stock of food storage that can last twenty-five-plus years, repackaging your own bulk dry goods at home is a great option. Food options for this process include dozens of bulk packaged ingredients such as dry beans, lentils, rice, wheat, and pasta. These items can be purchased in large 25- and 50-pound bags from a variety of retailers including:

- Costco.com
- SamsClub.com

- LDS Home Storage Centers (See the locations link at the online resource page for this book: CreekStewart.com/disasterready.)
- HarmonyHouseFoods.com
- CountryLifeFoods.com
- Amazon.com

In all cases, the packages these products come in are not suitable for long-term storage. They must be upgraded to ward off pests, moisture, oxygen, and sunlight. This repackaging process can be done at home with minimal resources. Following is a complete overview of this process, which will set you up for success. If you're interested in a detailed look at all aspects, you can find that in my book *The Disaster-Ready Home*, available wherever books are sold.

The items you'll need to repackage bulk food products at home include:

- 5-gallon plastic buckets with lids
- 5-gallon Mylar food-grade bags
- 2,000cc oxygen absorbers
- 3-foot section of two-by-four lumber
- Vacuum or shop vac
- Home iron

Mylar is perfectly suited for long-term food storage because it is less permeable than plastic alternatives to gases such as oxygen. It is also moisture proof. The shiny silver bags used to package chips and snacks are Mylar. The open end of Mylar bags can be bonded together with a home iron. Oxygen absorbers are used to absorb any remaining oxygen once the bag is sealed. These are sized for the container being used, and it's recommended to use a 2,000cc absorber for 5-gallon buckets.

Start by lining a 5-gallon plastic bucket with an empty 5-gallon Mylar bag. Fill the bag with a bulk food product such as dry beans but leave 4–6 inches of space at the top. Open a 2,000cc oxygen absorber packet and drop it in the bag. Press the top of the bag closed and lay it over a section of two-by-four resting across the top of the bucket. Use a home iron set on high to seal the top of the bag. Stop sealing within 2 inches of one side and use the hose of your

Use a 5-gallon bucket and Mylar bag to repackage bulk dry goods.

vacuum or shop vac to suck out as much air as possible. Then, remove the hose and use the iron to seal the final 2 inches.

Once you get the hang of it, several buckets can be filled and sealed in just a few minutes. Oxygen absorbers normally come several to a package, so try to plan for using them all once you open a package. Or simply put more than one in a container. Otherwise, they will absorb their full amount of oxygen in a few minutes and be worthless.

It may surprise you to learn that the US Food and Drug Administration allows a certain amount of insect parts to be in bulk dry goods. For example,

225 insect parts are allowed to be in 225 grams of dry macaroni. When packaging your own dry goods at home, you can bet there will be insect parts and eggs inside your dry goods. Two effective ways to deal with this are freezing the food and/or mixing it with diatomaceous earth. After packaging my own food at home, I put the buckets in a deep freezer for two weeks. This will kill some, but not all, insect eggs.

Diatomaceous earth consists of the fossilized remains of tiny, single-cell organisms called diatoms. These crushed skeleton parts can be mixed evenly through dry food at the ratio of 1 cup per 50 pounds. If insects with exoskeletons hatch, the crushed skeletons of these diatoms cause the insects' exoskeletons to fail, and the insects die. This sounds crazy but is true. Look for food-grade diatomaceous earth, which is considered safe to eat. Between adding oxygen absorbers, freezing the food, and mixing it with diatomaceous earth, you'll have a good chance of not opening your dry oats, like my friend, and seeing a mass of moving larvae.

A Suggested Long-Term Plan

Every person and household is different, and everyone's long-term food storage plan is and should be different. Many factors can affect a plan, including the number of people in the household, their ages, diet restrictions, allergies and sensitivities, and more. For this reason, there is no "one size fits all" long-term food storage plan or schedule. I'd like to share with you my personal plan in hopes that it will help you outline one of your own. To make it more manageable, I've broken down my long-term food storage into three timelines. I've outlined each timeline and the plans I have in place for each.

ZERO TO TWO WEEKS
During this period, my plan is to consume all the perishable goods we keep in a two-week rotation in the refrigerator, freezer, and kitchen pantry. I intentionally keep two weeks' worth of our regular meals on hand for a two-week emergency.

TWO WEEKS TO THREE MONTHS

If an event should interrupt the food supply chain for more than two weeks, many other areas of preparedness will require my attention. These may include construction, home and neighborhood defense, childcare, and first aid. I want my meals during this crucial phase of survival to be as easy and simple as possible. For this reason, I have built up a three-month supply of freeze-dried food for my family. This is a combination of entrée meals, meat buckets, fruit buckets, and vegetable buckets. If I have water, I can easily feed my family during this time.

THREE MONTHS TO ONE YEAR

For this period, I have stored dry bulk goods in 5-gallon plastic buckets using the process I outlined earlier. These are food staples such as beans, lentils, rice, flour, salt, sugar, and more. Beans and rice together make a complete protein, and many people across the globe have subsisted on this type of meal for very long periods of time. Simple additions can prevent appetite fatigue.

Pet Food Storage

For those with pets, you'll want to make sure to consider them in your long-term food preparation. Many pet foods are high in oil content and do not store well using the Mylar bag and plastic bucket method. For this reason, I recommend slowly building a rotation stock for your pets. Most pet food has a shelf life of at least six months. Calculate how much pet food your animals consume each month and build a rotation stock to feed them for a period of time you feel comfortable with.

But just having food on hand for everyone, pets included, isn't enough. You must have a means to cook and prepare the food if the grid is down. Let's discuss a few options.

Off-Grid Cooking

Electricity is almost always interrupted during large-scale disasters. Natural gas failure isn't as common but certainly possible, such as in the case of earthquakes. Those who use propane to cook at home will be limited by how much they have in their tanks. It is important to prepare for cooking off the grid. There are several options here, including barbecue grills, camping grills, wood-burning fireplaces, and fire pits. However, I believe one option to be superior to all others. It is used by millions of people across the world in underdeveloped countries where electricity and fuel are scarce or too expensive: a simple stove called a rocket stove.

There's a reason rocket stoves are used for cooking in places with few resources. They are one of the most efficient cooking stoves in the world, and they require far less fuel than a traditional open fire or fireplace. In fact, most rocket stoves can easily cook a meal or boil water using just a handful of small sticks and twigs.

The design of a rocket stove is simple and ingenious at the same time. Fuel burns in a small combustion chamber and pipes the heat to the cooking surface through an internal chimney. It is so efficient in burning fuel that there is very little ash to clean up afterward. In addition, it is a nearly smokeless stove, making it discreet as well. Rocket stoves can be operated in small spaces such as a back porch or even a balcony. They do need to be located on a noncombustible surface, but the footprint is very small.

While there are countless different rocket stoves on the market, one of my favorites is from a brand called EcoZoom. At just over 1 foot tall, it is a powerhouse of an off-grid stove. It's made from cast iron, stainless steel, and sheet metal with ceramic insulation. It weighs about 15 pounds, and it's proven to be effective in dozens of countries around the world in the most trying of conditions. The cooking surface is also wok compatible which is nice for stir-fry meals. Like most small rocket stoves, the EcoZoom stove can quickly boil water or cook food using just small sticks and twigs that can be found in nearly any green space. You can purchase an EcoZoom rocket stove for around $150. Find a link at the online resource page for this book: CreekStewart.com/disasterready.

The EcoZoom rocket stove is a powerhouse of an off-grid stove.

Because of their simplicity, rocket stoves are also easy to make. In fact, you can make an incredible rocket stove in your backyard using just twenty-five bricks or pavers and a couple of old grill surfaces. You could purchase or source these supplies in advance and keep them in storage just in case you ever have a need to build a rocket stove. This is a skill I teach step-by-step in *The Disaster-Ready Home* book, but I also have a video on how to make one; you'll find the video listed at the online resource page for this book: CreekStewart .com/disasterready.

The biggest issue for most off-grid cooking options is fuel. Whether that fuel is natural gas, propane, or split wood, once the fuel is gone, cooking stops. This becomes a real problem in an off-grid emergency when your very life may

You can build a rocket stove in your backyard using just twenty-five bricks.

depend on the ability to boil water or cook meals. One of the biggest advantages of using a small rocket stove is the type and amount of fuel it uses. Rocket stoves work best when using sticks and twigs that are the diameter of a finger by just a foot long. These can be found almost anywhere including backyards, parks, and wooded areas and as driftwood at the edges of creeks and streams. They can also be split from scrap wood such as shipping pallets or old furniture. Just a small stack can be used to cook a full meal for an average family.

Because of the rocket stove's low cost, simplicity, efficiency, fuel economy, footprint, and even portability, it is the number one off-grid cooking solution I suggest to most people. Even if you have a more complex option in place, it makes sense to have a rocket stove as a backup to your backup.

For some reason, most people think about food first when it comes to at-home preparedness. While food is certainly a human survival need, it's not at the top of the list. Even more important is water. Not only is water necessary to cook most food, but the average person needs a minimum of 1–2 gallons of water each day for hydration and personal hygiene as well.

A Personal/Family Preparedness Plan is incomplete without considerations for water. These include but are not limited to freshwater storage, water purification tools, and a long-term plan for sourcing more water. The next chapter will cover everything you need to know about preparing your home if a disaster should interrupt your normal water supply.

CHAPTER 5

WATER STORAGE, PURIFICATION, AND SOURCING

It is said the average human can live for three days without water. According to an article at MedicalNewsToday.com, "A person may go from feeling thirsty and slightly sluggish on the first day with no water to having organ failure by the third." Dehydration quickly affects every bodily function including but not limited to mental clarity, dexterity, fine and gross motor skills, digestion, and sleep. Lack of water can make an already bad disaster scenario worse.

But access to water doesn't alone solve the problem. The water must be potable. Drinking water contaminated with human sewage, biological organisms, dead animals, or hazardous chemicals can make you sick and even cause death if medical help isn't available. Dehydration from diarrhea is the leading cause of death in the world, and the reason is bad water.

Water in Disaster Preparedness

A wide range of disasters, both natural and man-made, can pollute or interrupt your normal water supply. Power failures can cause well pumps and municipal pumps to fail. Earthquakes can bust water lines; winter storms can freeze them. Hazardous spills can pollute water sources. The list goes on and on.

These are just some examples of how quickly disaster can disrupt your normal water supply. Water is critical for not only hydration but also cooking, hygiene, cleaning, and sanitation. You might be shocked to learn how much water you currently use every day, between drinking, cooking, showering, flushing the toilet, washing dishes, and washing clothes. According to the US Environmental Protection Agency, each American uses an average of 82 gallons of water per day at home. In America at least, we take access to clean water for granted. This mentality lulls many to believe that preparing to live without it isn't necessary. That is a grave mistake.

Preparedness in the water department requires action in three areas: First is freshwater storage. Second is purification and filtration. And third is sourcing more water. This chapter will cover the basics of all three.

Strategies for Water Storage

Water is bulky and heavy to store. Just 1 gallon weighs roughly 8.3 pounds, and 5 gallons, 41.5 pounds. Water is also one of the most space-consuming items to store. This is why a renewable water source and a system for purification and filtration is so important.

Let's use a family of four as an example. With the amount of 2 gallons per

Store-bought water can be stored in the floor of an armoire.

person per day of water storage, just one week's worth of water equals 56 gallons of water—or over fifty 1-gallon jugs. That's a lot of water, and it's just for one week! I suggest keeping two weeks' worth of freshwater storage on hand for your family if possible. This can be done using one or a combination of the following storage methods.

STORE-BOUGHT JUGS OR BOTTLED WATER

Store-bought jugs or bottled water is one of the easiest forms of water storage. Cases of water stack nicely in closets, basements, or garage corners. They last at least a year without needing to purify or filter the water and are fairly economical especially if you catch a sale. It is very easy to line the bottom of a closet with cases of bottled water and cover them with cardboard or a piece of plywood to create a false floor. This becomes fresh water hidden in plain sight. There are countless creative storage areas for bottled and jug water.

MEDIUM-SIZED WATER CONTAINERS

There are dozens of food-grade and BPA-free water storage containers on the market. These range in size from 2.5 gallons to 7 gallons and are popular in the camping industry. One of my favorites is the 7-gallon Reliance Products Aqua-Tainer. Similar containers can be found on *Amazon* and at Walmart, REI, and many other outdoor retailers. Make sure they are food grade and BPA-free. Most square and rectangular varieties are stackable and fit perfectly in corners of basements and garages. They also have optional spigots for easily distributing the water into smaller containers. When full, they can weigh over 50 pounds each, and while they might be too heavy for some people to lift, they are a fantastic option for many people with ample space.

I recommend Reliance Products' 7-gallon food-grade water storage container.

LARGE-SIZED WATER CONTAINERS

If you have the space, large-sized containers can be a one-stop-shop option for you. Containers can range from 35 gallons to 500 gallons. I keep a 305-gallon

Food-grade 55-gallon plastic drums are the most available and affordable large-sized container option.

tank in the corner of my garage, as well as several 55-gallon plastic drums of water. Food-grade 55-gallon plastic drums are the most available and affordable large container option. They can be purchased on *Amazon* and even at hardware stores like Lowe's and Home Depot. Prices change constantly in this category, but an online search for "large water tank" will yield ample results. I have also listed some of my favorite options at the online resource link for this book: CreekStewart.com/disasterready.

One of the biggest considerations when it comes to large containers is weight. A 55-gallon drum of water will weigh in excess of 450 pounds. My 305-gallon tank weighs almost 3,000 pounds. Large tanks must be placed on solid surfaces. Ideal places are concrete slabs or foundations in either a basement or a garage. Racks can be built to hold large containers outside, but they must be built by someone who knows what they are doing. Tipping or falling 500-pound containers of water are extremely dangerous and can cause injury or death, not to mention potential water damage.

A drum pump, either manual or battery powered, that screws into one of the bungholes on the top of a 55-gallon plastic drum can be used to access the water inside. The pump has a pipe that reaches to the bottom of the drum and a hose on the outside that allows you to direct the water into smaller containers. For other large containers, make sure there is a spigot valve on the bottom side of the container that you can either attach a hose to or use to fill smaller containers. Most 5–7-gallon square plastic water containers have a spigot that screws onto the main cap as well.

A drum pump can be used to access the water inside a 55-gallon plastic drum.

Water Quality Maintenance

One of the most common questions I'm asked is how long stored water will last. Maintaining water quality has to do with many different factors.

My first suggestion might seem obvious: Only store water in containers made for storing water. Many people wash and recycle 2-liter soda and juice bottles for water storage containers. If washed thoroughly, these can be used. But in my opinion, it's not worth the time and hassle. One-gallon jugs of water are very affordable and a better option. Using them instead of reusing 2-liter bottles eliminates the risk of sugar residue promoting bacterial growth and your water tasting like grape soda. For water storage, never reuse any container used to store milk or toxic chemicals.

When it comes to any other used container, small or large, I recommend resisting the temptation to save a few dollars unless you know with 100 percent certainty that the container has only been used for water storage. The risk of leaching chemicals, flavors, and anything else from used storage containers is not worth the money saved, even if what was stored in the container was a food grade. Look for deals, wait for sales, and buy new.

According to the Environmental Protection Agency, regular household bleach (6–8.25 percent sodium hypochlorite) can be used to disinfect water at the ratio of two drops per 1 liter. Adding this amount when storing water will increase shelf life, depending on your water source and storage conditions. City tap water will contain residual chlorine as a purifier, but well water can be stored as well. I add the recommended amounts of bleach to my stored water as a precaution. However, if you have purification and filtration systems in place (discussed in the next section), you can always make your water safe to drink unless it's been tainted by toxic chemicals such as gasoline or pesticides. Never store your water near these types of chemicals, and if they have been spilled on the floor, then place a couple of two-by-fours beneath your storage container to prevent leaching into your water.

I replace and refresh my stored water every three to five years. If you store water outside in heat and sun, I'd suggest rotating at least every six months to one year. Storing outside is not an option for four-season climates due to freezing.

Regardless of which size container you use, the ideal storage conditions are similar to those of food. The best scenario is a temperature-controlled (50°F–70°F) place void of moisture, sunlight, and pests. Millions of people in the world live in areas where water isn't safe to drink, such as in South America. These people rely on deliveries of fresh water, which is stored in large tanks often on top of their house or a nearby tower in full sun. It may be necessary for you to store your large water tanks outside as well. Since your water will not be in constant rotation, you'll want to choose a black- or dark-colored tank to block out the sun and prevent the growth of microorganisms and algae. I've seen algae bloom in whitish tanks in as little as two weeks. Storage uphill, on a raised foundation or on a sturdy rack/tower built for this purpose, can allow you to gravity flow your water from a large tank into your home.

Lastly, it's important to clean your storage container at each water rotation. The easiest way to do this is with a power washer and a little soap.

Signs that your water might be contaminated include a cloudy appearance; visible sediment; a brown, orange, or discolored hue; visible algae growth; an oily film on top; or a metallic taste. Your water should be clear and odorless (a slight chlorine scent is possible if you've treated it). If you follow the guidelines and suggestions I've provided, you'll likely have no issues with water quality.

Purification versus Filtration

I once asked my grandpa whether a snake we saw in the yard was venomous. His answer was simple: If you don't know, it's venomous. I take the same approach with water in a disaster scenario. I treat all water as if it is contaminated. That is why there is a second layer to water security. This layer involves backup methods of purification and filtration.

While the terms *purification* and *filtration* are often used interchangeably when it comes to treating water, they are not the same, and it's important you understand the difference. Generally speaking, purification is more thorough than filtration. Filtration is the act of running water through a barrier of some kind that "catches" impurities. In most cases, filtration does not remove toxic chemicals and viruses. Purification, however, removes and/or kills impurities and often includes using chemicals, such as chlorine, to achieve this result.

The Big Berkey is one of my favorite tabletop water filters.

Rather than getting bogged down with terminology, let's discuss a few methods of purification and filtration that you should consider as your second layer of defense in disaster water treatment.

GRAVITY-FED WATER FILTER

You should not depend on a water filter that requires power, electricity, batteries, or any kind of water pressure. This includes reverse osmosis systems. Your disaster water filter should be gravity fed. Two of my favorite tabletop gravity-fed water filters are the Big Berkey and the ProOne. Both are similar in design and have an upper reservoir where the questionable water is poured and a lower holding tank with a spigot that holds the filtered water. Both also have a filter that acts as a sieve as the water drips from the upper to the lower tank. While each has its own proprietary filter, they both filter out an impressive list of contaminants. The ProOne, for example, filters out volatile organic contaminants, trihalomethanes, pesticides, heavy metals, disinfectants, herbicides, pharmaceuticals, fluorinated organic acids, parasites, algae, microplastics, and microbiological and radiological contaminants. (You can see a full filtration report for each on its respective website: ProOneUSA.com and USABerkeyFilters.com.)

Many households already use such systems to filter the pharmaceutical, chemical, and fluorinated contaminants out of the tap water they drink every day. Tabletop gravity-fed filters like these are the perfect solution for filtering questionable stored water in the containers mentioned earlier. If you live near a pond, river, or stream, these filters can also make that water safe to drink. In addition, you can filter rainwater through them. Having a filter like this on hand is an absolute necessity in every disaster preparedness plan.

Renewable Water Sources

In addition to freshwater storage and a reliable gravity-fed water filter, you will need to identify and secure a renewable water source. This is the water you will drink and use after your freshwater storage has been consumed. A renewable water source is one that you can go to over and over again to get fresh water.

The EarthMinded DIY Rain Barrel Diverter and Parts Kit makes a 55-gallon plastic drum a very effective rainwater harvester.

Even if it requires purification or filtration, you must have a renewable water source.

Renewable water sources can include nearby ponds, streams, or rivers. They can also include a well, cistern, or nearby spring. You can check FindASpring .org to see if there is a freshwater springhead near you.

If you don't have a renewable water source within walking distance of your home, you may want to consider implementing a rain barrel specifically designed for collecting water during a disaster. For this, I recommend using a 55-gallon plastic drum and purchasing an EarthMinded DIY Rain Barrel Diverter and Parts Kit. This kit contains all the pieces, including hole saws, you'll need to quickly and easily set up a 55-gallon drum as a very durable and effective rain harvester. These pieces attach to one of your existing gutter downspouts in about 30 minutes. You can even keep a barrel and parts kit in your shed or garage to deploy when necessary if you don't want a permanent rain barrel or you have a city or homeowners association that prevents it. You can also plan on using one of the 55-gallon drums you currently use for water storage. The kit costs roughly $40 and is a perfect renewable water source solution for everyone except those living in extreme arid regions with little rainfall.

Even though rain itself is safe to drink without purification or filtration, rain that falls on your roof, gushes through your gutter, and dumps into a rain barrel may harbor contaminants. For this reason, any drinking water from a rain barrel should be filtered using one of the previously mentioned gravity-fed filters. If such a filter is unavailable, there are a few other options to ensure that the water is safe to drink.

Alternative Water Purification Methods

Although a gravity-fed filter is highly recommended, it's important to also know two other simple and effective water purification methods.

PURIFYING WATER BY BOILING

Boiling water will kill microbiological organisms such as bacteria, protozoa, and viruses. It will not, however, remove chemicals, heavy metals, herbicides, or other contaminants from the water. The Environmental Protection Agency recommends boiling water for at least 1 minute to kill organisms. In altitudes greater than 5,000 feet, boil for 3 minutes. If the water is murky or filled with visible debris, it is wise to filter the water before boiling. This can be done with a coffee filter or even a T-shirt.

PURIFYING WATER WITH HOUSEHOLD BLEACH

Not only can household bleach be used to treat water for storage, but it can also be used to kill harmful microbes. The ratio is two drops of 6–8.25 percent sodium hypochlorite bleach to 1 liter of water. (Just remember that you must be "21" to drink—2 drops per 1 liter.) Do not use bleach with added scents. Be aware of concentrated bleaches and reduce the amount if necessary. You must wait for 30 minutes for the bleach to be effective, and the water cannot be cloudy or dirty. The water should be clear to start with, so prefiltering may be necessary.

Alternative Water Sources

Some other last-ditch water sources worth mentioning that could be available to most homeowners include the following:

- **Hot Water Heater:** Most hot water heaters contain 35–50 gallons of potable water. A drain valve can be opened at the bottom of the water heater to access the water inside. Be careful if the water is still hot. You can also attach a hose to the drain spigots.
- **Lower-Level Water Pipes:** Lower-level water pipes may still contain water even if there isn't water pressure. They can be cut open to drain the water inside. Be sure to shut off the main in case the water supply is reinstated.
- **Canned Goods:** Liquids in canned goods such as green beans and fruits can be drunk as is.
- **Swimming Pools, Spas, and Fountains:** While it's not a good idea to drink water from these sources due to its chemical content, the water can be used for cleaning, hygiene, and sanitation.
- **Toilet Tanks:** The water in the tank portion of a toilet can be used if you haven't added a disinfectant puck to the tank. Do not use water that has reached the bowl of the toilet.

CHAPTER 6

HEAT AND TEMPERATURE CONTROL

For those who live in four-season environments, cold temperatures are a concern that must be addressed. Cold is not only dangerous from a first aid perspective, but it also makes many other aspects of managing the effects of a disaster more difficult. The goal of this chapter is to introduce a variety of ideas to stay warm when your normal means of heat is interrupted. It'll begin with very simple and low-tech improvised solutions and also provide a list of updates you may want to consider to make your home more efficient.

Low-Tech Strategies to Stay Warm Without Power

Oftentimes, expensive or complicated solutions lead to inaction. For that reason, I've listed here several very simple and inexpensive solutions that can help you and your family stay warm if the grid goes down.

HOME SURVIVAL SHELTER

In his online course "Survive the Storms" at OutdoorCore.com, Chris Gilmour introduces the concept of a home survival shelter to stay warm in an emergency. In wilderness survival education, there is a cold weather shelter called a debris hut. The concept is simple: Create a small space surrounded by thick layers of

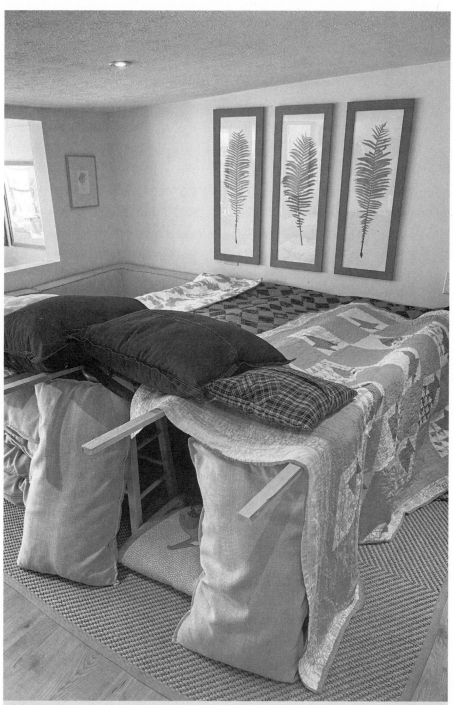

My family and I built an indoor "debris hut" around the couch using various household insulation items.

forest debris such as leaves and pine needles. The debris provides both a barrier from the cold weather and insulation to trap body heat inside the small shelter. It is a simple and effective design that has saved many lives in the wilderness.

Similarly, you can build an indoor "debris hut" using blankets, sleeping bags, pillows, and furniture in a room inside your home. This solution is especially good if you have children. What kid doesn't want to spend the night with their parents in a pillow fort?

The floor should be lined with a mattress or thick layer of blankets for insulation. Chairs and furniture can be used to create the framework and walls around the sleeping area. The roof can be made from boards, crutches, skis, broom handles, or any other rafter structure that is long and sturdy. The key is to keep the interior space small to trap as much body heat as possible. Once you've sized the interior sleeping space, the goal is to pile as many insulative things on top and around the shelter frame as possible. These could include clothing, blankets, pillows, jackets, towels, stuffed animals, and even rugs. You'll be surprised at the amount of insulation you'll find around the house. A thick blanket can be used for the door.

Once finished, this indoor debris hut can be a sanctuary of warmth. The body heat from two or three family members will keep a shelter like this toasty warm even in freezing temperatures. If you have pets, bring them inside with you! Building an indoor debris hut can help children get their minds off the disaster and focus on something fun and productive. To see a free preview video of Chris teaching how to build an indoor survival shelter, visit the online resource page for this book: CreekStewart.com/disasterready.

HOT WATER

If you have the means to heat water, then you have the ability to make one of the most effective low-tech warmers available. (A backyard rocket stove [see Chapter 4] would be the perfect tool for heating water!) Start by heating water in a pot. It's not necessary to bring the water to a boil; that would be too hot. Then, pour the water into scrap plastic or metal bottles. Two-liter soda bottles work perfectly for this. One of these bottles tucked under blankets or into a sleeping bag will provide warmth for hours and can stave off even the coldest temperatures if the heat is out.

IMPROVISED PORTABLE MASS HEATER

As a wilderness survival instructor, I've taught thousands of people how to heat hot rocks in a fire and use those rocks as mini mass heaters to keep themselves warm all night long. If you have a metal bucket, some sand, and a few softball-sized rocks, you can make one of the most effective small space heaters known to man.

Start by putting the rocks directly into a fire. This can be a fire outdoors or a fire inside a fireplace. Be sure the rocks are completely dry and have not been sourced from a wet area such as a creek or stream. Moisture inside the rocks can cause them to explode. While the rocks are heating, pour a few inches of sand into the metal bucket. Once the rocks are scalding hot (some will even turn red), use a pair of tongs or a metal shovel to place a few in the bucket on top of the sand. Then cover up those rocks with another layer of sand. Repeat this process until the bucket is full of sand and hot rocks. If the bucket is too heavy, you may only want to fill it halfway. Then, set this portable heater in a room on a noncombustible surface such as a concrete paver or tile floor.

The hot rocks will heat the sand, and the entire unit will radiate heat for many hours. Rocks and sand hold heat for a very long time, and your hot rock mass heater will easily cut the cold in a small room during a grid-down scenario. This allows you to build a fire outside but bring the heat from the fire inside. It's an incredible improvised solution that requires very few resources.

IMPROVISED TOILET PAPER ALCOHOL STOVE

If you're like many other preparedness-minded people, you're already stocked to the brim on toilet paper. This is an opportunity to put that mountain of TP to work in a different way. Years ago I was introduced to a small improvised stove consisting of just a 13-ounce metal coffee can, a smashed roll of toilet paper, and a bottle of 90 percent rubbing alcohol.

You start by kneading one roll of toilet paper and then removing the cardboard roll in the middle. Next, squeeze the roll together and twist it into the 13-ounce coffee can. It should fill the can entirely. Finally, slowly pour the bottle of 90 percent rubbing alcohol onto the toilet paper roll and let it soak in. It will take a few minutes, but you should be able to pour in the full bottle. Once the alcohol is fully soaked into the toilet paper, use a match or lighter to ignite

You can improvise a stove using a metal coffee can, smashed roll of toilet paper, and bottle of rubbing alcohol.

the top of the toilet paper. The alcohol will ignite, and you'll see a flame burning on top of the toilet paper.

A stove like this will burn for 12-plus hours on a single bottle of alcohol. When you notice the edges of the toilet paper starting to burn and turn black, that's your signal to blow out the flame and pour in as much alcohol as the toilet paper will hold. Then relight the stove and repeat.

Not only will this stove produce heat, but you can also use it to cook food, make coffee, warm soup, or heat drinks such as tea. Warm drinks and warm food go a long way to keeping you warm as well! Small alcohol stoves are very popular among hikers and backpackers and have been used for decades to cook meals on the trail.

Be sure to place this stove on a noncombustible surface such as an upside-down metal pot. One other safety note is that this stove will produce carbon monoxide (CO). Carbon monoxide is an odorless, colorless gas formed by the incomplete combustion of fuels. When people are exposed to CO gas, the CO molecules will displace the oxygen in their bodies and can lead to poisoning and even death. My recommendation is that these be used in a well-ventilated area and not a cramped small room. The addition of a carbon monoxide detector in your home is also prudent.

BLANKET BLINDS, WALLS, AND DOORS

When my mother was born in rural Kentucky, the family farmhouse was not yet finished. In fact, several exterior walls were made from handmade quilts. The fact that my mom's family survived the winter in a house with quilt walls is a testimony to the effectiveness of this common emergency recommendation!

Keeping a small space warm is much easier than keeping an entire house warm. Isolating activity and sleeping in a small insulated room can be a very valid strategy to keep your family warm. Thick blankets and quilts can help you do this. Blankets can serve as doors and as additional walls to divide a large space into a smaller living area. You can also prevent heat loss from windows by covering them with blankets.

Blankets and quilts are a drastically underestimated resource when it comes to disaster preparedness. If you have the storage space, stock up on as many as you can fit. Invest in wool if you have the budget.

HAND AND BODY WARMERS

This option may not heat your home, but it will sure make a difference under the covers, in your jacket pockets, and in your shoes. These small air-activated hand and body warmers are the perfect solution when you need to cut the chill in extreme cold.

Small warmers like these heat up by a process called oxidation and are activated when they are exposed to oxygen once the package is opened. Most have a shelf life of three years, so keep this in mind when storing them for emergencies. They are also a fantastic addition to vehicle emergency kits and come in different sizes for hands, feet, and even the entire body.

Hand and foot warmers are activated when exposed to oxygen once the package is opened.

Off-Grid Heat Options

Sometimes the best solutions require you to rewind the clock and revisit what your ancestors did just a few decades ago or take notes from what people are currently using in remote areas. In this section you'll find off-grid heat options that are simple and effective.

KEROSENE SPACE HEATERS

Once chopping and splitting wood became too difficult for my grandmother and grandfather, they switched to heating their home with small-footprint kerosene space heaters. Three of these heaters heated their entire home during the long winter months in Indiana.

Make sure to use a kerosene space heater like this one away from anything flammable.

Kerosene space heaters like those my grandparents used are still available and popular today. You can find them at most home improvement stores for around $150. Unlike gasoline, kerosene will store for five-plus years without having to add fuel stabilizers. Kerosene is also a multifunctional fuel that can be used in hurricane lamps for light and some simple stoves for cooking. At one time, kerosene was a very popular cooking fuel in America.

There is a fire risk to kerosene heaters, so make sure to keep them on a noncombustible surface and away from anything flammable like drapes or furniture. In my experience, heaters of this type will burn for roughly 8–12 hours on a 2-gallon tank of 1-K kerosene. You can use these numbers to calculate how much kerosene you might want for storage.

MR. HEATER PORTABLE BUDDY HEATERS

These portable Buddy heaters are very popular among hunters and outdoor enthusiasts and are one of the most popular portable heaters in America. They are also safe for indoor use and use propane as fuel. Unlike virtually any other fuel, propane can be stored indefinitely. This is a huge plus when choosing this heater as a backup source of heat.

The heaters in the Buddy series come in a few different sizes and accept standard 1-pound screw-on tanks of propane. One of these tanks will heat a 225-square-foot area for over 5 hours. An optional hose and connections kit can be purchased to attach these heaters to a 20-pound propane grill tank, which will drastically extend the heating time.

Not only can one of these tanks heat a room, but it is a perfect option for helping warm a specific area such as an area where pipes may freeze. At less than $150, this is a viable small-scale backup heat option for people on a tight budget. Learn more about these heaters at MrHeater.com.

A portable propane heater is safe for indoor use.

VESTA SELF-POWERED SPACE HEATER AND STOVE

The VESTA space heater by InstaFire is a small-footprint off-grid heater that can be used to warm up a room and also cook or boil water. It uses chafing fuel cans for heat. You've likely seen chafing fuel cans under

The VESTA Self-Powered Space Heater and Stove is perfect for people who live in an apartment.

food on a catering line keeping the food warm. Chafing fuel is an odorless fuel that's safe for indoor use.

The VESTA also has a built-in fan that's powered by heat from the cans. Three cans of fuel will safely heat a 200-square-foot room for hours. This is one of the easiest small-scale backup heating options available on the market today and is perfect for people who live in an apartment or other small space. You can find a link to the VESTA at the online resource page for this book: CreekStewart.com/disasterready.

A wall-mounted ventless heater can heat up to 1,000 square feet of space.

VENTLESS PROPANE OR NATURAL GAS HEATER

If you have a large propane tank or natural gas for fuel, a fairly simple and inexpensive backup heating solution is a ventless gas heater. *Ventless* means that you don't have to vent the heater outside or have a chimney. These heaters can be either wall mounted or free-standing and have a direct gas hookup to your propane or natural gas fuel source. Once installed, they are simple to operate and can heat between 500 and 1,000 square feet of space. They are a great backup heating solution.

WOOD-BURNING STOVE OR FIREPLACE

At the time of this writing, my family and I are living in a small, 800-square-foot cottage. When I first bought this home in my twenties, it had a grid-tied electric-powered natural gas furnace. One of the first preparedness decisions I made was to install a small wood-burning fireplace. I chose a cast iron fireplace from a Norwegian company, Jøtul. For $1,200, the local dealer

A wood-burning fireplace is a backup for me and my family when the power goes out during a snowstorm.

delivered and installed it for me in the corner of the sunroom. Now, when the power goes out during a winter snowstorm, we fire up the wood-burning Jøtul fireplace to heat the house, make coffee, and cook meals.

Many people think installing a wood-burning fireplace is a big decision, but it doesn't have to be. If you have a spare corner or open exterior wall, chances are you can install a freestanding fireplace very inexpensively. In Scandinavian countries, it's not uncommon to have several small fireplaces throughout the home.

Having access to wood is a bonus but not a necessity. Conduct a search online for firewood delivery and store the firewood in a protected place in your yard or next to your shed. Store as much as you have space for. Cover it with a tarp and it will last for years. While I'm a fan of the previously listed off-grid heating options, there's nothing quite like a wood-burning fireplace when the grid goes down.

Insulation, Weatherproofing, and Home Updates

In addition to some of the simple and inexpensive warming and heating options previously mentioned, there are several actions you can take that will prevent heat loss and make your home more efficient in cold (and warm) weather.

CHECK YOUR INSULATION

Attic and wall insulation can make a drastic difference in preventing heat loss. If you suspect that you have poor attic or wall insulation, you can contact a local insulation provider to get a quote on beefing up either or both. Spray-foam options can even be used to fill your exterior walls through holes drilled from outside the house. It's an amazing process.

UPGRADE YOUR WINDOWS AND DOORS

Windows are the number one point of heat loss for a home. Upgrading existing windows to more efficient models can go a long way in reducing heat loss. The same is true with doors. I once visited a friend in Minnesota during the winter and was surprised to see his windows were covered on the inside with a clear plastic sheet. It was then that I learned about cold weather shrink-wrap window film. It is an inexpensive strategy for improving window efficiency in cold weather. If upgrading windows doesn't fit the budget, purchase a window film shrink-wrap kit. The process is simple. First, apply double-sided tape around the window frame. Next, place shrink-wrap film over the window and secure it to the tape. Lastly, use a hair dryer to heat and tighten the film. It's a very slick process that traps an insulative layer of dead air between the film and the window. I now help my parents do this each fall to several large older windows in their home with great success.

INSULATE YOUR GARAGE DOOR

Swapping out your garage door for a more energy-efficient insulated version can make a big difference in temperature control. I did this in my last home and couldn't believe the difference in the winter. I replaced our old cheap single-layer wooden garage door with one filled with foam insulation, and it was a very good decision.

ADD WEATHER STRIPPING

Leaks around windows and doors are a prime culprit for heat loss and infiltration of cold air. Take a minute to identify drafty windows and doors and apply good-quality weather stripping around them to stop leaks.

HANG THICK CURTAINS

Each fall, my mom would take a full Sunday to change out the "summer curtains" for the "winter curtains." The winter curtains were made from two thick layers of fabric and designed specifically to provide an extra insulation barrier between our home and the cold windows. We can learn a lot from the "old ways" people used to do things.

SEAL AND INSULATE OUTLETS AND SWITCHES

Believe it or not, heat can escape through your wall-mounted outlet and switch boxes. An easy and inexpensive fix is foam inserts designed specifically to seal these up tight. Duck Brand makes a Socket Sealers Universal set that I've used and like.

Final Thoughts on Heating

If you haven't noticed yet, there is no perfect off-grid heating solution. All come with pros and cons. My response to this is that *any* solution is better than *no* solution and any decision is better than indecision. Choose one that best fits your circumstances and take action.

Not long ago, nearly every home in America was heated using a wood-burning fireplace. In just over a century, we have transitioned to a people dependent on electricity. Data from the US Census revealed that about 41 percent of US households were heated with electricity in 2022—and I suspect it's even more now.

If complete self-reliance is the goal, then you must be able to live without electricity or generate your own power. Going completely off the grid is another book for another day. However, the next chapter will discuss a few options for you to consider when it comes to generating your own power short term.

CHAPTER 7

POWER GENERATION AND BACKUP

According to the US Energy Information Administration, US electricity customers averaged 7 hours of power interruptions in 2021. When the grid goes down, self-sufficiency regarding power becomes your lifeline. This chapter will stress the importance of having reliable power generation and backup systems in place for disaster scenarios.

In full transparency, I've studied and even experimented with going off the grid using solar power. I've concluded that it is not a viable and practical option for the average person. It is simply a commitment to self-sufficiency and preparedness that most people are not prepared for or willing to make. For that reason, you won't find a suggestion in this book to fill your backyard with solar panels and cut your ties to the power company. Instead, this chapter will offer practical solutions for choosing and setting up systems that can provide essential short-term electricity during temporary disaster-caused power outages.

The Role of Power in Emergencies

Electricity is in the crosshairs of nearly every natural and man-made disaster. Power outages come in all shapes and sizes. A winter storm can affect just one neighborhood, but a larger event can affect an entire region. Power outages have a compounding effect. The longer power is out, the worse things get, and the more people are impacted. Loss of power has the fastest and greatest impact on society's most vulnerable. These include older people, people with disabilities, the sick, and children.

On the level of an apartment dweller or a homeowner, losing power can mean some or all of the following: loss of heat, light, refrigeration, hot water or even water, communications, Internet connection, Wi-Fi, ability to run medical equipment, and ability to charge devices, as well as stalled sump pumps, inactive sewage grinder pumps, and more.

On a larger, macro level, entire infrastructures can be affected. These include city communications, water pumps, transportation, retail businesses, grocery stores, gas stations, ATMs, banks, restaurants, and delivery services. Food spoilage and water contamination start immediately. Medical facilities and nursing homes will have to rely on backup power, if available, to run critical medical equipment. After Hurricane Katrina ravaged areas of Mississippi, Louisiana, Alabama, and Florida, it took six weeks before the power in all affected areas was restored. That's a month and a half without electricity!

For most people, setting up a long-term backup power supply, such as a fully integrated solar charging system, isn't practical or in the budget. However, there are several options worth considering that can provide short-term power and/or intermittent power for powering and/or charging critical systems.

Portable Gasoline- and Diesel-Powered Backup Generators

Portable gasoline- and diesel-powered generators are the low-hanging fruit of backup power options. Affordable and easy to operate, they are available for purchase at many different retailers, including home improvement stores such as Lowe's and Home Depot. You can expect to pay $500 and up for a good gas-powered generator.

These generators are priced according to wattage. The higher the wattage, the more powerful the generator and the more devices it will power. To give you an idea, an average home can be powered by a generator that can provide 5,000–8,000 watts of power. All gas-powered generators must operate outside because of carbon monoxide exhaust. You can power your home with this style of generator using two options: extension cords or a transfer switch.

A small, portable gas-powered generator can be purchased at a home improvement store.

If you are using extension cords, you simply start your generator outside and run extension cords through an open door or window to the appliances or devices you need to power. However, this method has drawbacks. Not only is it messy, but using the wrong-sized extension cord can also be a fire hazard. If using this option, I recommend purchasing what's called a generator cord, or gen-cord. This is an extension cord specifically designed to distribute the power from a generator. It plugs directly into the 20- or 30-amp plug on the generator, and you just have to run one cord into your home. The other end of the gen-cord splits into several standard 120-volt outlets where you can plug items. With this option, you can only power items that you can plug into an outlet.

Alternatively, you can have an electrician install what's called a power transfer system or power transfer switch. This switch ties directly into your home electrical panel and allows you to send power to not only outlets in your home but also appliances like air conditioners, furnaces, ovens, and ceiling fans. A special type of gen-cord runs from your generator through a slightly open window or door and plugs into a receptacle on the transfer switch to send power. This is a more integrated approach to providing your home with power.

Reputable sources for power transfer switches are Generac, Reliance Controls, and EcoFlow.

Whether you choose the extension cord method or the transfer switch option, gas-powered generators have one big drawback. You must have fuel to power them. Most portable generators will run 4–15 hours on one tank of gas, and this is highly variable depending on the model, size, and load. If you're considering this option, you will need to test your generator to see how long it will run on one tank of gas and then calculate how much gas you'll need to have on hand to power it for an ideal amount of time.

Stationary Propane- or Natural Gas–Tied Whole House Generators

This option of backup power has exploded in recent years. This style of generator is hardwired to your home electrical panel and is designed to kick on as soon as power is interrupted. These generators typically run on either propane or natural gas. They require a natural gas feed or a large propane tank in order to operate.

As you might imagine, hooking one of these up is a job for a professional, and you can expect to spend $6,000 or more for the generator and installation. These generators also require yearly maintenance to keep them running in tip-top shape, typically for an extra fee. Some electrical cooperatives have generator programs to help make buying one a little easier. Call your local electric company and see if they have any incentives or provide installation.

The advantages of these generators is that they provide backup power for almost your entire home. Natural gas is one of the most reliable fuels during a disaster, and if you have a propane tank, you can run this type of generator for a long time, especially if used intermittently. The disadvantages are that you're still dependent on fuel and the unit and installation are pricey. This type of generator is also huge, so it's not an option for apartment dwellers and others who live in tight quarters in a city.

A large propane tank (seen in the background) fuels my Generac whole house generator.

Portable Solar Generators and Power Stations

This is one of my favorite backup power categories because the energy is renewable. Unlike gasoline, diesel, propane, and natural gas, renewable energy isn't depleted once it's used. Two types of renewable energy are solar and wind. I'll only be discussing solar in this book.

There have been some incredible advancements in this category in the past decade. The capability of solar generators has gone up while the size and price have come down. An example of this is the Jackery Explorer 3000 Pro Portable Power Station. With just over 3,000 watts of power, this 63-pound unit can power most homes. It's also portable, so it can be taken on the road to power an RV or off-grid camp. There is an optional transfer switch that connects to your home breaker box and allows you to quickly and easily transfer power from the power station to your grid. This particular unit charges by using solar panels, direct current (DC) from a vehicle, or by plugging into a wall outlet. It takes 3–4 hours to charge by solar panels and about 2½ hours to charge by a wall outlet. At the time of this writing, the price of the base unit is $2,500–$3,000 but can exceed $7,000 with an added transfer switch, and six 200-watt solar panels. This is the same price (or less) for what you can expect to pay for a propane or natural gas generator to power a whole house.

Many different companies make solar generators. Jackery is just one. Others include Goal Zero and EcoFlow. The portability of these units is very attractive. If you ever had to evacuate, which we discuss in detail in Part 3 of this book, having portable power could be a big advantage. I have a small, 240-watt Jackery power station that I use to charge my cell phone, power my laptop, and keep my camera batteries charged while I'm traveling. It uses one solar panel and does the job perfectly.

If you live in a sunny area, a solar generator might make a lot of sense for you. If you live somewhere that's cloudy and rainy all the time, then keep in mind that the sun is your fuel when it comes to solar power generation.

If you're in the market for a larger, more robust grid-tied or off-grid-capable solar-powered whole home energy system, be prepared to pay upward of $50,000. For recommendations that will save you time and money, go to the online resource page for this book: CreekStewart.com/disasterready.

The Bare Minimum: Battery Power Bank for Tools and Devices

From batteries and flashlights to ham radios and toys, almost everything is rechargeable these days. I remember in the past needing to have a suitcase full of batteries to charge all the electronics in our home. Now we just need a couple of different USB charging cords. This presents a huge opportunity for those smart enough to prepare for disaster.

Being able to charge these electronics while off-grid is critical to any disaster preparedness plan and should be a bare minimum goal when working through the power generation and backup portion of your plan.

It used to be that one would have to understand how to build a small solar-powered system to charge these items. But now, a small and compact portable solar station from a company like Jackery can charge almost any battery-powered electronic device you can think of. One of the smaller solar generators can be purchased for under $300 and charged by just one plug-and-play solar panel. These small generators have built-in inverters, USB plugs, and even 110-volt outlets to make using them very straightforward.

I use a small Jackery solar generator to power my rechargeables during a disaster.

You'll want to take inventory of your electronics and make an effort to purchase rechargeable versions or at least rechargeable batteries to power them. Examples of tools and devices that are very useful in any disaster scenario include but are not limited to:

- Flashlights
- Two-way radios for communications (detailed in Chapter 8)
- Ham radios

- NOAA-capable radios for weather and disaster updates
- Toys for children
- Portable small power banks for taking on the go to power cell phones
- Lanterns
- Bicycle lights if using a bicycle for transportation (discussed in Chapter 14)

In addition, you should consider collecting an assortment of tools powered by 18-volt (or higher) batteries, along with extra batteries and chargers. Some brands, such as Ryobi, manufacture a staggering assortment of tools that can all be powered from the same rechargeable battery. Being able to use tools in the midst of a crisis has obvious advantages. Following is a list of tools in the Ryobi lineup that use the same 18-volt battery:

- Drill
- Circular saw
- Jigsaw
- Reciprocating saw
- Weed eater
- Chainsaw
- Blower
- Inflator
- Shop lights
- Vacuum
- Sump pump
- Vehicle jump starter
- Nail gun
- Pole pump
- Power washer
- Pole saw
- And dozens more!

With a handful of 18-volt rechargeable batteries, a solar power generator, and an assortment of tools, you have the ability to do a lot of work, day or night, even when the grid is down. This is a power generation category with amazing potential that many people overlook.

My battery charging station includes the following items:

- Small Jackery solar generator
- 200-watt solar panel
- Power strip
- Two 18-volt battery chargers
- Six 18-volt batteries

I recommend collecting an assortment of rechargeable 18-volt battery-powered tools.

- USB charging cord organizer with a dozen or so USB charging cords for various devices including cell phones, headlamps, and more
- Two-way radio charger
- AA battery charger with rechargeable lithium batteries
- Anker portable rechargeable power bank

In addition to tools, a battery charging station allows you to charge critical communications devices such as two-way radios, ham radios, and cell phones. Whether you're communicating security messages within your neighborhood network, sending messages to loved ones, or calling for rescue, history tells us how critically important communications is during and after a disaster. It is a preparedness category that many people ignore. I believe this is due to not clearly understanding the available options. In the next chapter, I'll outline what you need to know in order to maintain effective communications during and after a disaster.

CHAPTER 8

COMMUNICATIONS

Your ability to communicate can often mean the difference between life and death. Unfortunately, normal methods of communication are often among the first services to be interrupted. This is one of the factors that contribute so greatly to the overall chaos of disaster.

In many disaster scenarios, entire networks of off-grid emergency communications need to be deployed to help organize rescue and recovery efforts. Traditional landline, cellular, and Internet communications are usually interrupted and temporarily useless to survivors when they need them most. In many disaster-recovery situations, it has been independent ham operators, mostly volunteers, who reestablish a lifeline of communications amid the chaos.

But connecting those inside the disaster area to first responders is only half of the communications equation. Communications among those inside the disaster zone is critical as well. This chapter will discuss communications during and after a disaster.

The Two Categories of Communications

There are essentially two categories of communications during and after a disaster. There is communication *inside* the disaster zone and communication *outside* the disaster zone. While some methods of communications can certainly do both, it's important to understand the importance of being able to communicate to and from each zone.

First, there is the issue of communicating with those in your close circle, such as family members and neighborhood friends. These are people who are also directly affected by the crisis. They are with you at ground zero of the disaster and, like you, may also be temporarily cut off from the outside world. It is critical that you have an off-grid way to communicate with these individuals. These critical communications include sending and receiving security messages, locating family members, keeping track of team members, sharing resources, and monitoring local first aid efforts and updates regarding rescue teams, incoming resources, news from the outside world, and more.

Communication inside the disaster zone is tied directly to the Family Communications Plan introduced in Chapter 2 and will be detailed later in this chapter. Independent, battery-operated, off-grid methods to communicate with those close to you inside the disaster zone are critical to managing and navigating the crucial hours or even days after a disaster.

In addition to localized and family communications, sending and receiving messages outside of the disaster zone is vital. When cell phone and Internet communications are off-grid, other options are critical to coordinating emergency communications between first responders and those affected by disasters.

Without emergency communications organizations such as Amateur Radio Emergency Service (ARES) and Radio Amateur Civil Emergency Service (RACES) and volunteer ham radio operators, disaster areas and everyone affected could be cut off from all outside communication for days or even weeks. It is not an exaggeration to say that organizing rescue efforts is impossible without these backup off-grid methods of communications. These systems and those who operate them are the unsung heroes of almost every large-scale disaster in recent history.

The Cell Phone and Internet Dilemma

In general, the world communicates via cell and Internet communications. Whether it's to family members overseas or neighbors down the street, we pick up our cell phones to call, text, or email a quick and instant message. The reliability of these three options has become incredibly impressive over the past few decades, even in remote areas of the world. Just a few years ago, I trained with a remote community of indigenous Paipai people in the mountains of Baja California, Mexico, and was shocked not only that I had cell service but also that they used cell phones. The recent advent of satellite Internet has extended this reach even more.

Such unparalleled reliability is a double-edged sword. It lulls us into believing that this level of connectivity will always be available when we need it. However, millions of disaster victims in recent years can attest to the fact that none of those methods of communication will be there when you need them most.

These are not forms of disaster communication. They weren't designed to be, and they don't operate by the same rules. Like first responder services, they were not designed to withstand the stressors, malfunctions, and overwhelm that come with disasters. Optimal performance depends on optimal circumstances, and there is nothing optimal about times of crisis.

Because of this, cell and Internet communications cannot be and should not be considered a primary communications tool for disaster preparedness. If they work, consider it a luxury. If they do not, consider it expected and be ready to deploy one of the off-grid communications options detailed in the sections that follow.

Introducing Ham Radio

Amateur radio, also known as ham radio, is the best option for disaster communications. This isn't just my opinion but also the opinion of tens of thousands of other professionals around the world. One such expert is my friend Joe Bassett of ValiantOutfitters.com. Joe is an outdoor instructor as well as a ham radio operator who has been deployed to provide amateur radio (ham radio) emergency communication during a number of hurricane scenarios.

In addition, Joe has helped hundreds of individuals pass the ham radio license exam using his online study course, Ham Cram, which can be found at OutdoorCore.com. When it comes to disaster preparedness communications, Joe is the man to ask for advice.

Because Joe is an expert in this field, I've asked him to outline why the ham radio is the best device for disaster communications. The criteria he uses for his decision are:

A ham radio is the best device for disaster communications.

- **Portable:** Walkie-talkies are hands down the most portable type of two-way radio. Along with portability comes ergonomics. A radio that's too large and heavy is a pain to carry around on a belt or in a bug out bag (discussed in Chapter 13). But if it's too small, the controls can be hard to manage, especially for large or gloved hands. Also, the smaller the radio, the less real estate for buttons and controls. This leads to multilevel menus, which are counterintuitive.

- **User-Friendly (with Training):** This is one place where "channelized" radios with fewer frequencies might have an advantage over ham radios. These are the basic walkie-talkies you find at your local sports store. With flexibility comes complexity. This is why earning a ham radio license is important. Practicing with ham radio after you have your license ingrains knowledge into your head. Sure enough, the Federal Communications Commission (FCC) isn't going to care about licenses in the midst of disaster, but using a ham radio takes experience and practice. And practicing needs to happen before a crisis. It's illegal to practice transmissions on a ham radio without a license, so get your license and be prepared. The good news is that earning your ham radio license isn't that hard and can help overcome the more complicated features of using a ham radio.

- **Rugged:** This feature is important for outdoor, camping, and harsh environments such as encountered in disaster relief or survival situations. To rate ruggedness, we'll refer to the IP (ingress protection) code for electronic devices. The IP code is an international standard that rates a product's protection against intrusions by water and foreign particles.

- **Receives NOAA Weather Radio and the Emergency Alert System (EAS):** Whether it's a hurricane approaching landfall in the Southeast, a thunderstorm squall line with tornadoes barreling across the Midwest, or tsunamis threatening the Pacific coast following an earthquake, NOAA Weather Radio is where to turn for the most accurate information. Along with NOAA Weather Radio is the EAS. The EAS is the voice that says, "This is a test, it is only a test…"; if it's a real emergency, they'll announce impending weather or other information. While some non-ham radios also include this feature, it is a capability on all ham radios.
- **Accesses Multiple Radio Frequencies:** Ham radio can receive analog signals from services such as first responder, aviation, and marine radio frequencies. And, with some modification, it can transmit on these frequencies as well. (Please remember that using a ham radio on non-ham frequencies is allowed only when there is imminent danger to life or limb.)
- **Allows Two-Way Communications:** Yes, CB, Family Radio Service (FRS), General Mobile Radio Service (GMRS), Multi-Use Radio Service (MURS), and marine VHF radio are all two-way communications. They're also available for general public use. However, compared to ham radio, they are limited in transmission range, frequency range, or both. Ham radio allows two-way communications, permits operations on numerous frequencies, and is long range capable.
- **Ensures Operational Security (OPSEC):** Many preparedness-minded individuals are concerned with operational security. Keeping looters, bandits, human predators, and others in the dark as to activities is a distinct advantage. While none of the radio systems discussed here has National Security Administration (NSA)–level encryption, which is illegal on public radio services, most of them provide rudimentary protection against accidental discovery of the ham radio operator's location.
- **Long Distance Capable:** This one gets tricky because more power doesn't necessarily mean more distance. All things being equal, ham radios can transmit over a greater radius than FRS, GMRS, and MURS (keeping

in mind that walkie-talkies are best for portability). The most useful frequencies in tactical and survival situations propagate by line of sight. That means the two radio antennas need to "see" each other to transmit over the longest distance. Non-licensed radio services (CB, FRS, etc.) are limited to a mile or two under usual circumstances. By comparison, two people of average height can easily communicate across 3–5 miles using a ham walkie-talkie.

- **Affordable (Less Than $200 Each):** You'll need a minimum of two radios, and more if you outfit a team or neighborhood watch crew. Expense is an important consideration, and under $400 for two-way communications is reasonable. Yes, there are some ham radios that are less expensive. But they all fail in one or more of our criteria. Most ham radios that are under $100 fail in durability. They're fine and fun radios when conditions are good, but I wouldn't bet my life on them. These budget radios might be a third of the price, but you'll replace them five times over the life of a more robust radio.

So which ham radio does Joe recommend? It's called the Yaesu FT-60R, and it fulfills all the previous criteria. Joe's FT-60R has faithfully served as his primary walkie-talkie for every one of his deployments. He literally bets his life on it. Following are the details about this radio's criteria:

- **Two-Way Communications:** The FT-60R is not just a receiver. It allows for two-way communication.
- **Portable:** Measuring in at 2.3" × 4.3" × 1.2" and weighing just 13.03 ounces, it fits easily in even a small hand, but the buttons and LCD screen are ergonomic for large fingers.
- **User-Friendly:** Manual programming is intuitive, and it can be preprogrammed with 1,000 memories.
- **Rugged:** The die-cast metal helps to ensure this unit can stand up to unfriendly conditions.
- **Receives NOAA Weather Radio and EAS:** The FT-60R is capable of an automatic search of weather radio frequencies and background scanning of alerts.

- **Accesses Multiple Frequencies:** The frequency range includes first responder, aviation, marine, and public (CB) radio services, and receiving these frequencies (except CB) is possible right out of the box. A modification can be done to enable CB transmission (note that nonemergency transmission is illegal). There is also an easy-to-use scan feature for these frequencies.
- **Ensures OPSEC:** The FT-60R includes Private Line (PL) tones that provide minimal privacy, but high-level operational security is not a feature of any ham radio. The FT-60R also has a feature called Enhanced Paging and Code Squelch (EPCS). EPCS allows you to "page" a particular station and only receive calls from that station. The FT-60R can also be password protected against unauthorized use.
- **Long Distance Capable:** At 5 watts maximum, the FT-60R can communicate well up to a 5-mile radius and even farther in certain conditions.
- **Affordable (Less Than $200):** You can find a link to this radio at the online resource page for this book: CreekStewart.com/disasterready.

Non-Ham Radio Communications

It's true, you must study for and pass an exam to get your ham radio operating license. It's also true that anyone you plan on conversing with via ham radio must also have their license. The idea of an exam or even the cost of ham radio can be a hurdle for many, especially those just looking to set up a more localized communications network among neighborhood friends or family members. I completely understand this. If that's the case, there are other options. They are inferior options to ham radio, but they are absolutely better than having no radio communications network at all.

There are several other forms of off-grid two-way communications, but my goal is to make your decision as simple as possible. For this reason, I will only discuss one other option: General Mobile Radio Service, also known as GMRS. The official FCC definition is this:

GMRS radios are plug and play right out of the box.

The General Mobile Radio Service (GMRS) is a licensed radio service that uses channels around 462 MHz and 467 MHz. The most common use of GMRS channels is for short-distance, two-way voice communications using hand-held radios, mobile radios and repeater systems. [GMRS also allows] short data messaging applications including text messaging and GPS location information.

Look at GMRS as a middle option between ham radio and FRS. FRS refers to two-way radios purchased at outdoor retailers. Notice that a license is required to operate GMRS radios. The good news is that there is no exam. You complete the online form, make a $35 payment, and the license arrives. One license covers an entire family, and this includes spouse, children, grandchildren, stepchildren, parents, grandparents, stepparents, brothers, sisters, aunts, uncles, nieces, nephews, and in-laws.

GMRS radios are less complicated than ham radios. They are plug and play right out of the box. They are small, portable, and easy to attach to a belt or backpack. GMRS radios are also more powerful than FRS radios. The result is more range. In perfect conditions, GMRS radios can access a range of 5–10 miles, while FRS radios are limited to 1–2 miles. GMRS radios also have access to repeater channels, which can boost range even more. GMRS and FRS operate on the same channels, and a GMRS radio can communicate with an FRS radio and vice versa.

If your goal is to establish a family-based or neighborhood-based communications network, GMRS can be a good option. Rechargeable models are available to be used with your off-grid battery bank.

If GMRS sounds like the best decision for you and your family, I have provided convenient instructions and links that walk you through the licensing process as well as links to recommended models at the online resource page for this book: CreekStewart.com/disasterready.

Having two-way radio is just one component to an overall plan. These radios are just a tool to help accomplish the goal of keeping lines of communication open among your family, your key team members, and the world outside the disaster. Now let's discuss what an overall Family Communications Plan looks like.

Family Communications Plan

As mentioned in Chapter 2, a Family Communications Plan is an outline of directives and information for how to get in touch with each other if you're at work, school, or away from home. It also contains a list of important contacts including phone numbers. This information helps family members communicate if normal methods of communication aren't working. Following are the elements you need to include in your emergency communications plan:

- A full list of emergency contacts, including the local fire station and police department and each family member, among other important emergency contacts. The contacts' phone numbers should also be entered into each person's cell phone. Also enter ICE (In Case of Emergency) numbers into your phone. These are emergency contact numbers that can be accessed by first responders just in case you are unconscious or injured. Enter the contacts as ICE-1-NAME. For example, in my phone, I have my wife entered as ICE-1-WIFE and my brother as ICE-2-BROTHER.
- An out-of-town contact, including address and phone number. This is a contact outside the local area who can be an alternate contact if local communication is unavailable.
- Three meeting places. These include (1) somewhere a safe distance from your home in the case of fire or something similar so that everyone can quickly be accounted for, (2) an in-town family meeting place if your home is inaccessible, and (3) an out-of-town family meeting place if access

to your home and in-town meeting place is blocked. Include the name and addresses of each place in your document. Examples are (1) a certain tree in your yard, (2) a community park or church, and (3) an out-of-town relative or friend's house.

- At a bare minimum, a set of GMRS handheld radios for local family communication or communication between neighbors. As discussed, GMRS radios can communicate over several miles and are a good option if cell phone service is interrupted. You are required to have a GMRS radio license to operate on this frequency, but the license is inexpensive and does not require an exam. I have included a link to the radios I recommend, along with a link to help you get licensed, at the online resource page for this book: CreekStewart.com/disasterready.

- The ability of the GMRS radios you purchase to be programmed to receive NOAA frequencies. Follow the manual for programming these frequencies into the radio. You can find the NOAA radio channels for your area at this link: Weather.gov/nwr/station_listing. If you don't buy GMRS radios, purchase a rechargeable weather radio to keep up with the latest alerts and weather information. A link to the one I suggest is at the online resource page for this book: CreekStewart.com/disasterready.

- A check to see if your local emergency management team has any alert services to sign up for. These may include text messages and email updates that they send out during a crisis. Use this link to find your state's emergency website and sign up for any alert systems they have in place: FEMA .gov/locations.

- Assurance that every family member has a printout of this communications plan and information in their wallet, purse, vehicle, and/or backpack.

As a part of America's PrepareAthon! campaign, Ready.gov has created a really well-done PDF of fillable cards for a Family Communications Plan, which I've made available for you to download at the online resource page for this book: CreekStewart.com/disasterready. Remember, communications is not just about staying connected to friends, neighbors, and family but also about ensuring safety and health in the midst of crisis.

CHAPTER 9

FIRST AID AND MAINTENANCE

There are few guarantees when it comes to predicting what will happen when a disaster strikes. However, first aid issues almost always come with the territory. According to the US Centers for Disease Control and Prevention (CDC), 44 percent of Americans do not have first aid kits in their home. That's a sobering statistic in normal times and a flat-out terrifying statistic if a disaster strikes. Whether it's mechanical injury triage or an off-grid breathing machine, you can expect first aid skills, resources, and knowledge to be in very high demand.

Ironically, this high demand causes complete overwhelm for medical first responders. Their systems are not designed to handle the influx of need associated with most disasters. Consequently, when you need medical attention most, it will likely be slow, inadequate, or altogether unavailable.

You must be prepared to provide yourself and your family with basic medical care using preexisting training as well as stocked tools, resources, and medicines. This chapter is not designed to teach you first aid skills. That is best done through hands-on training courses. Instead, this chapter will outline the categories of first aid skills in which you should become proficient. In addition, you'll learn about the bare minimum resources you need to have on hand in your disaster first aid kit to deal with injuries that may commonly happen in a disaster scenario.

Basic First Aid Skills

Let's first define first aid in a disaster scenario. The level of training and resources needed for disaster first aid is far beyond the scope of an over-the-counter first aid kit stuffed with Band-Aids and antibacterial ointment. I'll assume that you know how to apply Band-Aids and treat the most basic cuts, stings, and scratches.

Of the 56 percent of American households that have a first aid kit, I would suspect that most of these are basic over-the-counter kits made by a business whose primary goal is a high profit margin rather than truly valuable first aid tools. Most of these kits are useless and contain fillers that offer zero solutions to serious injuries. This chapter will provide you with a shopping list of first aid tools and gear that can make a huge difference when you need them. When I started in disaster preparedness training, my first aid kit was the smallest and least-expensive kit in my arsenal. As I've trained and gained knowledge and experience, it has grown to be one of the most expensive and extensive kits I own. The more you learn about first aid, the more you realize the importance of investing in training and gear.

Before we get into gear, let's first discuss a handful of first aid categories you should be prepared to address. This is by no means an exhaustive list, but it covers a wide range of injuries you may potentially experience and need to treat in a disaster scenario. Being prepared with advanced training and key tools and resources to deal with the following thirteen categories will cover many bases:

- **Trauma and Musculoskeletal Injuries:** Trauma injuries include broken bones and fractures, sprains and strains, head injuries, spinal injuries, dislocations, and crushing injuries. Immediate assessment and immobilization is imperative to prevent any of these injuries from worsening.
- **Shock:** Shock is a life-threatening condition when the body isn't getting enough blood flow. It can be caused by several different things including a heart condition, overheating, an allergic reaction, and more. Understanding how to recognize and stabilize a person until medical help is available is critical.
- **Bleeding and Wound Care:** This category includes bleeding control, wound cleaning and dressing, puncture wound care, and treatment of

lacerations and abrasions. The proper care of wounds can also prevent infection.

- **Burns, Scalds, and Radiation:** Sunburn, thermal burns, electrical burns, and chemical burns are all batched into this category. Treatment can involve cooling the area and applying appropriate bandages. Pain management is also important.

- **Respiratory Emergencies:** Asthma attacks, trouble breathing, and choking all fall under this category. Having the knowledge and training to mitigate these types of issues is critical. The Heimlich maneuver is a required skill in this category.

- **Cardiovascular Emergencies:** Cardiovascular emergencies deal with issues of the heart, such as heart attacks, irregular heartbeats, cardiac arrest, and more. Knowing CPR is a critical skill in this category.

- **Environmental Injuries:** These are emergencies caused by the environment, such as hypothermia, frostbite, heat exhaustion, and heatstroke. Knowing how to quickly recognize and treat these conditions is imperative to managing disaster injuries in extreme conditions.

- **Allergic Reactions:** Although allergic reactions may not be caused directly by a disaster, they can be fatal without prompt action. Having the tools on hand to mitigate anaphylaxis, insect stings, and food allergies is wise.

- **Toxic and Poisoning Exposure:** Whether from ingesting poisons, inhaling toxic substances released from a disaster, or coming into contact with hazardous materials resulting from a crisis, managing exposure can be critical in a disaster scenario.

- **Neurological Issues:** Seizures, strokes, and concussions can have debilitating and fatal consequences. Stabilizing a patient until medical attention can be reached is important to prevent long-term effects.

- **Eye Injuries:** Eye injuries can involve eye trauma and also objects or chemicals in the eyes. Having the tools to protect and wash the eye is important to preventing long-term damage or loss of eyesight.

- **Infection Prevention:** Not only are wound care skills and resources important to preventing infection, but having a store of antibiotics on hand is important as well.

- **Extraction and Transport:** This category involves building improvised stretchers and travois for moving or extricating a victim from a dangerous area to a more stable location for treatment.

I understand if the previous list seems like a lot. It is. But it's important to recognize that you may very well be the only help available in a disaster scenario. It is not uncommon for first responders to be entirely cut off from disaster zones and unable to reach injured victims for hours and even days. The best-case scenario is a very slow and delayed response from first responders. Your first aid skills could make the difference between life and death for your family or neighbors.

Formal Training

Doctors, nurses, combat medics, and EMTs study for years to be proficient in the previously mentioned categories. This knowledge doesn't come from reading a book or watching a video. In my experience it only comes from investing time and money in hands-on courses. The closest category of training I can recommend that covers these types of skills is what is known as wilderness first aid. This training is also sometimes referred to as wilderness first responder, wilderness medicine, or wilderness medic. These types of programs train you to handle common injuries in the wilderness, and many of those overlap with the types of injuries you'll see in a disaster scenario.

Many different wilderness first aid training programs are available. A Google search for "wilderness first aid training near me" will reveal many options. The list of organizations that follows also identifies reputable training in this area. (Additionally, I have provided direct links to the training courses at the online resource page for this book: CreekStewart.com/disasterready.)

- American Red Cross: RedCross.org
- NOLS: NOLS.edu
- REI Co-op: REI.com
- Scouting America: Scouting.org

In addition to these organizations, the following companies offer trauma medicine courses that would be an excellent option for training:

- **Refuge Medical** (RefugeMedical.com): Based in Oklahoma, Refuge Medical has a hands-on trauma medicine course titled "Refuge Responder." I've included the direct link to this training at the online resource page for this book: CreekStewart.com/disasterready.
- **North American Rescue** (NAReducation.com): North American Rescue offers a variety of both online and hands-on training courses. One of my favorites is an e-course titled "Bleeding Control Product Training," which provides instructional guidance through the use and application of several very important bleeding control products including the combat application tourniquet (C-A-T), emergency trauma dressing, wound packing material, and more.

The training programs available from these organizations cover many of the thirteen training areas previously highlighted. However, following is a list of specific medical skill sets that one should aspire to learn as a part of an overall disaster medical preparedness plan. This is by no means an all-encompassing list but certainly a highlight of important skills to practice.

- **CPR:** Used to restore blood circulation and breathing.
- **Heimlich maneuver:** Used to prevent choking.
- **Wound cleaning and dressing:** Includes emergency trauma dressing, wound packing, and use of compression gauze and clotting agents.
- **Fracture splinting:** Specifically, how to use a SAM splint.
- **Tourniquet application:** Specifically, how to apply a C-A-T.
- **Bandaging techniques:** Includes using a cravat, or triangular bandage, and an ACE bandage.
- **Recognition of shock**
- **Assessment of head and spinal injuries**
- **Administration of epinephrine:** Used to manage severe allergic reactions and anaphylaxis.
- **Burn dressing and management**
- **Recognition and treatment of hypothermia and hyperthermia**

- Eye injury management
- Poisoning/hazardous chemical management

Disaster First Aid

As previously mentioned, a disaster first aid kit isn't your typical over-the-counter first aid kit. In fact, it's not likely you'll find a sufficient disaster first aid kit at any common outdoor retailer. Most available kits are filled with Band-Aids and safety pins, neither of which is very useful in a true medical emergency.

When it comes to putting together a disaster emergency kit for you and your family, you ultimately have two options. First is to buy one from a specialty retailer that understands wilderness, disaster, and trauma medical needs. These kits don't come cheap, and you'll likely need to supplement them with items that address some of the categories mentioned previously. This option, however, saves a lot of time and also leverages the knowledge of experts to help pick out your medical supplies. A second option is to assemble your own medical supplies piece by piece from numerous suppliers. While this option may take more time and research, you only purchase the exact items you want and need.

Either way, I've included information that will help you. First, I'll list some reputable suppliers of robust disaster-ready first aid kits. Then, I'll break down a short list of supplies you should consider purchasing if you're building your own kit.

Disaster-Ready First Aid Kit Suppliers

While many first aid kit suppliers exist, I can only in good faith recommend those I know, use, and trust. Following is a short list of suppliers that know what they're doing and offer quality products you can count on when it matters most.

- **Refuge Medical:** Refuge Medical offers a wide variety of first aid kits that include trauma-centric items. You can choose from personal first aid kits to entire buckets of supplies. Their website is RefugeMedical .com, but I've also listed my recommendations at the online resource page for this book: CreekStewart.com/disasterready.
- **North American Rescue (NAR):** North American Rescue is a seasoned supplier of not only fully assembled kits but also hundreds of individual first aid products. You can shop their website,

Storing medical supplies in a cooler works well.

NARescue.com, and visit the online resource page for this book to see my highlighted recommendations: CreekStewart.com/disasterready.

Building Your Own Disaster First Aid Kit

Whether you purchase an existing first aid kit and wish to add to it or simply want to assemble your own from scratch, this section will prove very helpful. The following list of recommended items is one I've created through my own online and field training as well as advice sought from medical professionals, wilderness medics, and combat medics over many years. The items listed will help you treat and manage many first aid issues you might encounter during a disaster scenario. I've listed specific brands when applicable. I have also included this list, along with clickable shopping links to the specific products I recommend, at the online resource page for this book: CreekStewart.com/ disasterready.

Sterile Dressings and Bandages

- Various sizes of sterile gauze pads
- Rolled gauze bandages (different widths)
- Cravats, or triangular bandages (for slings and splinting): Large, ideal for splinting and bandaging and even as a makeshift tourniquet.

Adhesive Bandages

- Assorted adhesive bandages (various sizes; waterproof preferred)
- Butterfly bandages (various sizes)

I assembled my own disaster first aid kit from scratch.

Wound Cleaning and Treatment Aids

- Antiseptic wipes or solution (iodine or alcohol based)
- Hydrogen peroxide or saline solution (for wound irrigation)
- Antibiotic ointment or cream
- Sterile saline for eye irrigation

Blister Care Supports

- Leukotape: The "it" item for blisters; when used in conjunction with gauze to cover a blister, will stick to skin for weeks, even standing up to sweat and water from bathing; can also be employed for use as general medical tape.

Splinting and Immobilization Materials

- SAM splint: Can be used to splint any limb, but most importantly can also be utilized as a cervical collar for neck/spine injuries.
- ACE wrap bandages: Have a host of possible applications, including as a pressure bandage for a wound or as a tourniquet or rigged into a sling.
- Duct tape or medical tape

Blood Loss Stoppage Aids

- Pressure bandage, such as NAR Emergency Trauma Dressing
- C-A-T: Bleeding control for life-threatening injuries involving extreme blood loss.
- Combat Medical Celox Rapid Z-Fold: Wound-packing gauze with a hemostatic agent for clotting.
- Israeli Compression Bandage (6 inch): For emergency wound dressing.
- Compressed cotton gauze (4.5 inch × 4.1 yard—6 ply): Compact; ideal for wound bandaging and for wrapping injuries.
- Hemostats or clamps: To clamp blood vessels and assist with suturing.
- Sterile sutures/wound-closure strips: To knit skin together and facilitate healing of cuts.

Respiratory Supports

- CPR mask or face shield
- Pocket mask with a one-way valve
- Nasopharyngeal airway (NPA #28): The airway adjunct of choice for tactical professionals; used to keep the airway open.
- HyFin Vent Chest Seal: For use exclusively on deep chest wounds; prevents air from entering the wound while inhaling and allows air to escape during exhalation; features a fail-safe system that allows the vent to keep working even if it becomes clogged with blood.

Burn Care Aids

- Water-Jel burn dressing (4" × 4"): A sterile packet burn dressing sized to fit common burn areas like the palm or the back of the hand, the neck, and so on.
- Burn creams or ointments

Eye Care and Protection Supports

- iSHWASH: Fits on a standard water bottle and works as an eye-flushing mechanism.
- Polycarbonate Eye Shield (PES)

Medications

- Pain relievers (acetaminophen, ibuprofen)
- Antihistamines (for allergic reactions)
- Aspirin (for cardiac emergencies)
- Epinephrine auto-injectors (for allergic reactions)

Personal Protective Equipment (PPE)

- Moldex R95 Disposable Particulate Respirator: Keeps particulate, debris, dust, and germs out of the lungs.
- Eye protection (safety glasses or goggles)
- Disposable gloves

Documentation and Communication

- Waterproof notepad
- Sharpie marker
- Waterproof bags

Special Needs Items

- Prescription medications (if needed)
- EpiPen (for severe allergies)
- Inhaler (for asthma)

Miscellaneous

- Medical gloves (latex-free)
- Hand sanitizer or antiseptic wipes
- CPR instructions or first aid manual
- Emergency whistle
- Thermometer
- Multi-tool or utility knife
- Flashlight or headlamp
- Trauma shears: Can serve as a general cutting tool for myriad uses beyond cutting gauze or bandages.
- Tweezers or forceps: For removing anything embedded in the skin.

- Scalpel (with protective cover)
- Space blanket or emergency bivvy: Used to hold in body heat for warmth and potentially fight hypothermia.
- Insect repellent: For keeping away potential disease- or virus-carrying insects.
- Medicated/SPF lip balm: Used to heal and protect; lips are very susceptible to harsh weather conditions and extreme sunlight.

There are countless first aid books you can reference, but here are two manuals I suggest reading and having in your kit:

- *The Survival Medicine Handbook: The Essential Guide for When Help Is NOT on the Way* by Joseph Alton, MD, and Amy Alton, APRN
- *Where There Is No Doctor: A Village Health Care Handbook* by David Werner with Carol Thuman and Jane Maxwell

Disaster Antibiotics

Properly cleaning and dressing wounds can reduce pain and also the possibility of a bacterial infection. Bacterial infection, whether caused by a wound or something else, can be deadly in a matter of days if not treated right away with the appropriate antibiotics. For this reason, everyone should consider adding a full spectrum of antibiotics to their disaster first aid kit.

From bite wounds and exposure to anthrax to giardiasis and urinary tract infections, there are a host of reasons why one might need antibiotics in a disaster situation. Don't count on getting a prescription from your local doctor. Luckily, there are several companies that specialize in providing antibiotics for those preparing for disaster. One of my favorites is Jase Medical. They offer a product called the Jase Case, which includes the following five emergency antibiotics:

- **Augmentin:** Augmentin is a combination of the drugs amoxicillin and clavulanic acid in the form of clavulanate potassium. Amoxicillin is an antibiotic that fights bacteria, and clavulanic acid helps stop certain bacteria from growing and becoming resistant to amoxicillin. You can use augmentin to treat multiple types of infections such as skin, sinus, and urinary tract infections, as well as pneumonia, bite wounds, and intra-abdominal infections.

- **Azithromycin:** Azithromycin is an antibiotic used to treat respiratory infections, skin infections, ear and throat infections, some sexually transmitted diseases, and infectious diarrhea. It is often used when someone has a penicillin allergy.

- **Ciprofloxacin (Cipro):** Cipro is an antibiotic that is frequently used for people that have been exposed to anthrax or certain types of plague. It is also useful for other bacterial infections such as urinary tract infections, kidney infections, bone and joint infections, infectious diarrhea, typhoid fever, meningitis, and more.

- **Doxycycline (Doxy):** Doxy is an antibiotic that can be used to treat many conditions including skin infections, ear and sinus infections, pneumonia, and bioterrorism infections (like anthrax, plague, and tularemia). It is also useful for preventing malaria and for treating infections caused by ticks, mites, or lice. This antibiotic has been shown to treat some MRSA (methicillin-resistant *Staphylococcus aureus*) infections.

- **Metronidazole:** Metronidazole can be used for a number of conditions affecting the stomach, liver, skin, joints, and brain, including parasitic infections, skin infections, intra-abdominal infections, infectious diarrhea, tetanus, and sexually transmitted diseases.

You have the option to add on a huge variety of other medications as well. I have a direct link for you to use at the online resource page for this book: CreekStewart.com/disasterready.

Another excellent option is Duration Health, whose mission is to save lives by providing access to emergency medications and supplies. This company offers a wide variety of prescription medical kits that include common antibiotics and more. In addition to browsing these kits, I would highly recommend downloading their *Duration Health Field Guide*. This guide is an emergency medical reference covering over sixty prescriptions and over-the-counter medications. Written by Duration Health emergency physicians, it is for the layperson experiencing a medical emergency who is unable to access real-time medical care. This is a fantastic resource to print and include with your disaster survival library. I've put a direct link as well as links to my suggested kits from Duration Health at the online resource page for this book: CreekStewart.com/disasterready.

Prescription Medications

Besides antibiotics, each home likely has at least one prescription medication taken by a family member or loved one. These, too, must be taken into consideration when preparing your disaster first aid kit.

Those dependent on medicine to be comfortable, function, or live are among the most vulnerable during and after a disaster. For many, a missed dose of medication can be serious or even have fatal consequences. If this is true for you or your loved ones, you need to make plans to have a minimum of a one-month supply of all medications on hand as a disaster buffer.

Most medications have an expiration date of one year. Research suggests that these expiration dates are much longer, but it's important to abide by the expiration date on your medication. For this reason, the best approach is to enter your medications into a system of rotation, like the food rotation system discussed in Chapter 4. Rather than put extra medications into storage, where they will eventually expire, work the extra medication into your normal cycle. With rotation, you will always have extra medications on hand that will have approximately one year of shelf life left.

If you have not already done so, contact your prescribing physician and explain to them that you are preparing a disaster emergency kit and that you would like to have at least one month (or whatever timeline you want) of your medicine on hand. Given this explanation, they should have no problem with prescribing you an extra thirty-day supply.

In addition to prescription medicines, there are many other condition-related items that may need to be stored. These include but are not limited to syringes, colostomy bags, ointments, creams, child and adult diapers, pet meds, and more. It is imperative you take some time and make a list of all medical supplies you and your loved ones use on a regular basis and make sure to either store or put these items into a system of rotation.

Be sure to store any and all medical supplies in a clean, dry area out of the sun. They are susceptible to all of the same enemies as food, including oxygen, heat, and moisture. Also store all medications in their labeled child-proof containers out of reach of children. Storage in a waterproof container such as a camping dry bag or an old cooler works well for items that are not in rotation. These waterproof kits can also be quickly loaded into a vehicle if necessary for evacuation.

CHAPTER 10

PERSONAL PROTECTION AND SELF-DEFENSE

First aid issues resulting from a disaster are unfortunately not the only threat you face. History teaches us that disaster scenarios bring out the best and the worst in humanity. While thousands of volunteers come to a disaster zone to help the needy, criminals see disaster as an opportunity to exploit the vulnerable. In addition, desperate disaster victims seeking to provide for their own families may do desperate things. For this reason, you must also consider self-defense and home defense as key aspects of disaster preparedness.

In times of crisis, your safety can depend on your ability to protect yourself and your loved ones. This chapter will discuss why self-defense and home defense are important components during and after a disaster. In addition, you'll find practical strategies for ensuring personal safety in various emergency situations.

Understanding Disaster Violence

While most people rally together during a crisis, there is an inarguable uptick in crime. Most of these spikes occur with burglary and looting, sexual assaults, domestic violence, and fraud. The overwhelm of law enforcement and first responders makes tracking these surges in crime difficult. Response times are often slow or nonexistent if help can be contacted to begin with.

Women are especially vulnerable in times of disaster, especially if alone or caring for children and loved ones and unable to relocate to an area of safety. Research indicates that domestic violence increases dramatically in the wake of a disaster.

While there is much debate as to the specifics of how much a disaster affects crime, there is no debate that it does affect it, even if for a short period of time. If you or your family is caught in the crosshairs, one thing is certain: It will be up to you and your friendly neighbors to stop it. By preparing for a worst-case scenario, you'll have a better chance of diffusing, de-escalating, or defending yourself and your loved ones.

A Note about Self-Defense Laws

Laws surrounding self-defense can be confusing at best. The bottom line is that defending yourself and your family can have legal consequences, inside and outside of a disaster scenario. I cannot stress enough the importance of understanding your state's self-defense laws. These laws may affect how you prepare for and carry out an act of self-defense. To find your state's self-defense law, simply Google "[your state] self-defense laws" and many results will populate to educate you.

Self-defense laws generally fall into the following three categories:

- **Stand Your Ground:** You have no duty to retreat from a situation before resorting to deadly force when you have a reasonable belief that you are in danger; not limited to your home, place of work, etc.

- **Castle Doctrine:** A common law principle where you have no duty to retreat before using lethal force *if* you are in your home or yard (some states include a place of work and occupied vehicles).
- **Duty to Retreat:** You have a duty to retreat from a threatening situation and possibly leave it to law enforcement if you can do so with complete safety.

Regardless of your state's stance on self-defense, you need to thoroughly understand it. With that said, let's discuss some strategies, techniques, and options to both avoid and engage in a self-defense scenario.

Basic Self-Defense Strategies, Techniques, and Options

Like many preparedness skills, defense requires advance training. Whether it's use of firearms, martial arts, or pepper spray, the concepts are useless without having practiced them until they become second nature and instinctive. Following are some techniques and tools for you to consider working into your routine and training to prepare yourself for a moment that will hopefully never come:

POWER IN NUMBERS

One of the best self-defense tactics available is numbers. This harkens back to the importance of establishing community and a group of trusted neighbors before a disaster. Criminals will rarely choose to attack or engage a group of individuals. They prefer to choose vulnerable single or paired parties when given the option. Especially if you are alone or otherwise vulnerable (with children, older adults, people with disabilities), it is imperative to band together with neighbors if you suspect an uptick of crime in your area.

SITUATIONAL AWARENESS

Situational awareness simply means to be aware of your surroundings. This can and should be practiced every day until it becomes instinctive. Make an intentional effort to evaluate your surroundings while going about your normal day. Who is watching you as you walk from your car to the grocery store? Do you notice odd or sketchy behavior? Where are the exits in a restaurant? Is the area well-lit or dark? Are there other cars at the gas station when you pull up at night or is it vacant? Are you the only one entering a restroom? These are all very simple questions that you can get in the habit of asking yourself each day. Being situationally aware is very different from paranoia. Paranoia is when you're scared about what might happen. Being situationally aware is when you're prepared for what could happen.

STAYING HOME, ESPECIALLY AT NIGHT

A friend of mine's dad used to always say, "If you want to stay out of trouble, don't go out at night." Not only is this true in normal life, but it's also especially true in a disaster scenario. If you have not and are not evacuating outside of the disaster area, stay home. Avoid areas of activity where there is increased chaos, confusion, protests, desperate individuals, or heated personalities.

PERSONAL FITNESS

Let's face it, criminals are wired to prey on the weak and vulnerable. The less weak and vulnerable you can be and appear, the better. In preparedness, many people overlook the importance of maintaining your most valuable tool: your body. Like any tool that is not maintained, your body will not perform to the best of your ability when you're not eating right, exercising, and practicing self-care. Optimal health and strength can be your greatest self-defense allies. Your goal in life should be to become hard to kill, and this requires an intentional effort to fuel your body, mind, and soul with the best consumables you can find and afford. It also requires a no-excuses weekly exercise routine to strengthen your muscles and build endurance. Eating whole foods and cutting out unnecessary carbs, processed foods, sugar, colas, and seed oils will work wonders for your health, and simple body weight exercises can dramatically improve strength and endurance. I recommend a free downloadable phone app called Home Workout by Leap Fitness Group. It offers simple body weight exercise routines you can follow at home for just a few minutes each day.

MARTIAL ARTS TRAINING

Martial arts training is personal fitness taken to the next level. Regardless of the discipline, training such as Krav Maga, jujitsu, grappling, and boxing can prepare you to diffuse and/or confront an attacker. This type of training can drastically improve your outcome if ever face-to-face with someone whose intent is to harm you.

WEAPONIZED PERSONAL ITEMS

Consider the personal items you carry each day. Many can be replaced or improved to be nondescript weapons. Combined with some basic martial arts training, weaponized personal items can become impressive force multipliers. These include but are not limited to tactical pens, keychain Kubotans, tactical fighting canes, keychain fighting knucks (where legal), steel-toe shoes, and belts with heavy buckles. I once saw a video of a man defend himself against three attackers using his belt with its heavy buckle as an improvised mace. It was a surprisingly effective force multiplier.

My tactical pen could be an effective force multiplier in my defense.

STUN GUNS

Stun guns are very popular self-defense tools in America. They are inexpensive, easy to use, and very effective. You'll often hear the words *stun gun* and *taser* used interchangeably, but these devices are not the same. A taser is a gun-like device that shoots two metal prongs over several yards into an attacker's skin to provide an electrical charge. You've probably seen a video of a police officer shooting someone with a taser. I don't cover tasers in this book because they are expensive, finicky, and surrounded by laws in many states. Stun guns, on the other

The VIPERTEK VTS-989 stun gun is a bestseller.

Marking dye is a feature of SABRE Advanced Pepper Spray 3-in-1.

hand, don't shoot. They require direct contact and can deliver a high-voltage shock to disable an attacker. One of my favorite (and bestselling) stun guns is the VIPERTEK VTS-989. You can find a link to it at the online resource page for this book: Creek-Stewart.com/disasterready. Be sure to check your local laws and regulations regarding owning a stun gun.

PEPPER SPRAY AND MACE

Pepper spray is hands down the most popular nonlethal self-defense tool. Pepper spray is essentially tear gas in a bottle. When the trigger is compressed, the canister discharges a stream or spray that contains an inflammatory compound called capsaicin, which causes extreme pain and burning to the eyes. I recommend SABRE Advanced Pepper Spray 3-in-1; the SABRE brand is also used by the New York City and Chicago police departments and by US Marshals. (I've included a link to the product in the online resource guide for this book: CreekStewart.com/disasterready.) According to SABRE, 42 percent of attacks involve multiple assailants. Pepper spray can be very effective against more than one person by spraying them all. This model also has marking dye in the spray and a belt clip for easy carry. Some states do have regulations regarding pepper spray, so be sure to check local laws.

BYRNA LESS-LETHAL LAUNCHER

One of my new favorite less-lethal self-defense options is any one of the Byrna launchers. Byrna launchers are compact nonlethal personal security devices developed by Byrna Technologies Inc. They are one of the safest, most effective, and most reliable nonlethal self-defense weapons on the market today. They are easy to use whether you are a private citizen or a seasoned law enforcement professional.

A Byrna handheld launcher can fire a range of 0.68-caliber projectiles. These include environmentally friendly practice rounds, hard polymer (kinetic) rounds that can be used for training or self-defense, and chemical irritant rounds designed for self-defense. The chemical irritant rounds are engineered to burst upon impact, dispersing a cloud of powerful pepper and/or tear gas powder capable of disabling an attacker for up to 30 minutes.

The Byrna's compact size and line of custom-made holsters and carry bags make the Byrna easy to take with you wherever you go. Each Byrna launcher contains more than 100 precision parts and incorporates patented technology that allows it to operate very much like a real firearm. This is an excellent less-lethal alternative to a traditional firearm. Learn more at Byrna.com.

FIREARMS

There is no question that a firearm is the definitive self-defense option. Firearms are designed to neutralize a target. But in an untrained hand, a firearm can be more dangerous to the user and their family than the attacker. Unless you are willing to invest upward of hundreds of hours in firearms education and training, a firearm may not be for you. But with the proper training, there is no other more effective means of stopping an attacker in their tracks than the well-aimed placement of a high-velocity bullet.

There are essentially three categories of firearms to consider for self-defense:

- **Pistol/Revolver/Handgun:** Handguns are just that: Firearms that fit in your hand. They are easy to conceal and carry on your person (with proper permitting). Their range is typically 25–50 yards at most.

I keep a revolver at home for self-defense.

- **Shotgun:** Shotguns can be for either hunting or tactical scenarios. Many police officers carry tactical shotguns. They can fire a wide range of ammunition, from buckshot hunting rounds to large slugs. Shotguns are typically held with two hands up against the shoulder and, depending on the ammunition, are very effective from a short range up to 50-plus yards.
- **Rifle:** Like shotguns, rifles are held with two hands up against the shoulder. Some rifles can shoot accurately up to 1 mile, but most are designed to shoot 100–500 yards. These are not as well suited for close range as a handgun or shotgun, except Pistol Caliber Carbines.

There are many factors to consider when purchasing and choosing any type of firearm for self-defense. In all honesty, it is a topic for a book in and of itself. For that reason, I have provided a more detailed supplement that you can download at the online resource page for this book: CreekStewart.com/disasterready. This supplement is written by my friend Jess Alphin, who is a National Rifle Association (NRA) firearms instructor and NC-CCH instructor. In it, he discusses these three categories of firearms to help you make a more educated decision about what may be best for you and your situation.

If you do decide to purchase a firearm for self-defense, I also recommend purchasing self-defense protection from RightToBear.com. This protection offers you many benefits if you ever had to use your firearms in self-defense. These include criminal defense, civil defense, psychological support, and expert witness defense. Even in self-defense, shooting someone can have serious legal consequences, and it's important that you understand the laws of your state regarding the details of what is and what is not self-defense.

Security and Safety

Sometimes the best self-defense is home defense. There are numerous proactive measures you can take to:

- Deter criminals from approaching your home.
- Harden your home to prevent break-ins.

CRIME DETERRENTS

Deterrents are things you can do to make your home seem less of an ideal target in the mind of a criminal. These include but are not limited to visual and audible defenses. Following are a few options:

Dog

A large dog is one of the best crime deterrents available. But this option has the obvious drawback of all the responsibilities that come along with owning a dog. A second-best option is "Beware of Dog" signs and a dog-barking alarm that goes off when someone enters an area that triggers a motion sensor. (I've listed a few options for these at the online resource page for this book: CreekStewart.com/ disasterready.) Some alarms even get louder as the person gets closer to the house.

Outdoor Security Lights

Second to a dog, outside lighting is the next best crime deterrent. Because you're making plans for a disaster, I recommend choosing a solar security light option that does not require hardwiring to the grid. These have come a long way over the years with LED technology and have built-in solar panels and motion sensors that make them plug and play. They can be installed in under 10 minutes with a screwdriver or screw gun. Large solar streetlights are also available, which can be mounted on poles or trees to light up large areas, driveways, or parking lots. I've linked my favorites at the online resource page for this book: CreekStewart.com/ disasterready.

Solar security lights have come a long way with motion sensors that make them plug and play.

I take a set of doorstop alarms everywhere I travel.

Doorstop Alarms

Doorstop alarms look like simple doorstops. However, when in place and a door opens, the top presses down and an alarm sounds. They do not stop the door from opening but do give a warning that the perimeter has been breached. The loud alarm not only deters a criminal but also forewarns you to confront them or escape. I take a set of four of these everywhere I travel to quickly install where I am staying.

Motion-Activated Security Cameras

While most security cameras are grid tied, they can still deter a criminal. They can send alerts to your phone to notify you of activity and help you monitor what's happening in places outside that you can't see. The brands Ring and Blink are very popular and have a host of options.

Security Systems

There are significant drawbacks to a security system if the grid is down. First, it probably won't work. Second, if it does, response times will likely be much slower than usual. If the system is working, one advantage is the loud alarm triggered by a breach. This will not only deter the criminal but also give you advance warning to prepare for confrontation. Almost as effective as the system itself is the security system yard sign. Be sure to post your yard sign in a prominent area. You can also purchase these signs online at *Amazon* as visual deterrents.

Hardening Your Home

Home hardening comes in the form of added, updated, or reinforced physical barriers. Following are some of the most common and affordable ways to harden your home against forced entry:

REPLACING DOOR SCREWS

One of the best ways to harden an existing door to prevent prying or kicking entry is to replace all the short, 1- to 2-inch screws in the strike plate and also all the hinges with strong 3- to 4-inch screws that sink deep into the door jam. This is a very inexpensive and simple upgrade that strengthens the security of the door.

INSTALLING DEADBOLTS

A good-quality deadbolt is imperative for home security. Do not choose the least-expensive brand. Instead, pay more for a better-quality and more durable option. The Medeco Maxum Deadbolt has been honored by *Consumer Reports* as the strongest deadbolt across all categories, but it is expensive. Schlage deadbolts are also good options. If your door has glass windows or glass side panels within arm's reach of the deadbolt, you will need to use a double-sided deadbolt to prevent an assailant from breaking the glass and turning the deadbolt knob. Double-sided deadbolts require a key to lock and unlock on each side of the door. If you use a double-sided deadbolt, be sure to keep a spare key near the door but more than an arm's length away, just in case you need to quickly exit at night when the door is locked.

UPGRADING STRIKE PLATES

Most deadbolts come with a cheap surface–mounted strike plate. An easy $15 upgrade is the Battalion strike plate, which has four screw points and a full-metal recessed deadbolt cavity. This is a very simple way to boost deadbolt security. You can find a link to this at the online resource page for this book: CreekStewart.com/disasterready.

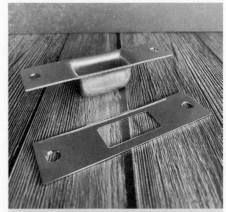

Upgrading a deadbolt's strike plate with this one from Battalion is a simple way to boost deadbolt security.

ADDING SLIDING DOOR AND WINDOW BARS

Adjustable jamming bars are one of the most effective ways to prevent entry through a sliding door or window. These adjust and jam between the sliding window or door and the door or window frame to prevent opening. There are many great options, and I have linked to some good ones at the online resource page for this book: CreekStewart.com/disasterready.

ADDING A DOOR SECURITY BAR

A door security bar jams under the doorknob and extends to the floor on the inside of the door. This is a quick and easy way to prevent someone from opening a door. Brinks Home makes an affordable version that I own and am happy with.

Adjustable jamming bars are one of the most effective ways to prevent entry through a window.

I'm happy with my affordable Brinks Home door security bar.

INSTALLING HURRICANE FABRIC

Break-ins aren't always caused by people. Hurricanes are notorious for sending debris through windows. Hurricane Fabric is a resin-coated hybrid fabric that provides protection from hurricanes. Hurricane Fabric delivers "full envelope" protection of your home and prevents the rapid pressurization of the building. This rapid pressurization is what causes roof liftoff and catastrophic damage. Hurricane Fabric not only blocks wind and rain but also protects against debris flying through glass windows. The fabric is sized for each window and fitted with special attachment fixtures. It's lightweight and easy to manage, unlike bulky plywood alternatives. Learn more at HurricaneFabric.com.

Protecting yourself, your family, and your property and possessions is a critical component to self-sufficiency. Many would argue that self-sufficiency isn't possible without the intent and ability to defend against those who may wish to thwart the plans, resources, and skills you've invested time, effort, and money into establishing.

CHAPTER 11

SELF-SUFFICIENCY OVERVIEW

Contrary to what many think, self-sufficiency doesn't require isolation. Instead, at the core of self-reliance is steadfast preparation and resilience. Preparedness is a result of action, and resilience is a mindset. Both are cultivated and developed over time. This chapter will give you an overview of self-sufficiency (both physical and mental) in the context of disaster preparedness. It'll focus on equipping you with the knowledge and skills needed to be independent and resourceful in various emergency situations.

The Concept of Self-Sufficiency in Emergencies

Whether it's food, water, alternative power, first aid skills, a Family Communications Plan, or one of countless other forms of preparation, those who strive for self-sufficiency fare better in a crisis than those who don't. In general, the more self-sufficient you become, the less you will be affected by a temporary or long-term disaster. This chapter will introduce as well as review several concepts to consider in your quest for self-sufficiency. I'll present some of these in checklist form to encourage action. You may be able to check off some of the listed items immediately. Others you'll want to start on right away. The remainder may become longer-term goals as you check more immediate needs off your list. Either way, self-sufficiency involves many facets, both physical and mental, and there is no straight line to the finish.

Preparing Your Home for Self-Sufficiency

To organize and review these items, I've divided the most important elements of self-sufficiency into ten main categories: shelter, medical training and supplies, heat, water, food, power, self-defense, communications, community, and evacuation. Items are arranged roughly in order of importance to help you quickly visualize where there may be gaps in your self-sufficiency efforts. Review the following checklists and decide which items you'll act on next. No list is exhaustive, but I've included plenty of options and topics to consider that suit a wide variety of families in a wide range of circumstances. Many of these topics have been covered in detail in earlier chapters of this book.

SHELTER
❑ Upgraded windows
❑ Upgraded doors
❑ Efficient window and door trim
❑ Window film kits
❑ Upgraded attic and wall insulation
❑ Upgraded garage door

- ❏ Disaster-specific preparations (Hurricane Fabric, wildfire remediation, sand bags, etc.)
- ❏ Battery-powered sump pump

MEDICAL TRAINING AND SUPPLIES

- ❏ Emergency supply of critical medicines
- ❏ Backup power source for any medicines that need refrigeration
- ❏ Disaster first aid kit built and available for use
- ❏ Specialized training on how to use the more technical first aid items
- ❏ Basic first aid knowledge such as CPR
- ❏ Stored supply of over-the-counter medicines, hygiene products, and personal protective gear

HEAT

- ❏ Backyard rocket stove for cooking
- ❏ Kerosene space heater plus fuel
- ❏ Propane space heater plus fuel for preventing water pipes from freezing
- ❏ Vented or ventless propane or natural gas heater or fireplace
- ❏ Wood-burning stove plus fuel
- ❏ Extra propane tanks for barbecue grill
- ❏ Backyard firepit with cooking tools/utensils
- ❏ Blankets

WATER

- ❏ One to two weeks of freshwater storage
- ❏ Gravity-fed water filter such as Big Berkey or ProOne
- ❏ Rain barrel kit plus 55-gallon drum for rain harvesting and garden watering
- ❏ Alternative renewable water source (pond, stream, river, spring, well)

- ❑ Water well with hand pump
- ❑ Large container for water storage (55-gallon drum or larger)
- ❑ Household bleach for water disinfection if necessary
- ❑ Metal pots and containers for boiling water
- ❑ Camping shower for taking a shower with water warmed over a fire or stove

FOOD

- ❑ Two weeks of rotation food storage (temporary)
- ❑ One to three months of long-term food storage (temporary)
- ❑ Raised-bed vegetable garden
- ❑ Vegetable garden in yard/on property
- ❑ Edible landscaping plants
- ❑ Indoor hydroponic garden
- ❑ Wild edible plants/foraging skills
- ❑ Food dehydrator for food preservation
- ❑ Harvest Right home freeze dryer for food preservation
- ❑ Traditional canning jars and supplies for food preservation
- ❑ Backyard chickens
- ❑ Livestock (guinea pigs, goats, pigs, cattle, etc.)
- ❑ Fishing equipment
- ❑ Map of nearby fishing locations
- ❑ Stocked private pond
- ❑ Aquaponics
- ❑ Bees for honey
- ❑ Maple trees for maple syrup
- ❑ Cricket farming (for food)
- ❑ Trapping equipment/knowledge/experience
- ❑ Hunting equipment/knowledge/experience

POWER

❑ Fuel generator (gasoline/diesel/natural gas/propane)

❑ Fuel storage (gasoline/diesel)

❑ Solar generator with solar panels

❑ Recharging station for battery-powered tools/devices

❑ Array of rechargeable tools/batteries/devices

❑ 18-volt tool assortment with charger plus batteries

❑ Whole-house solar power system

SELF-DEFENSE

❑ Firearm selection plus training and experience

❑ Nonlethal self-defense options plus training

❑ Security system/cameras/signage

❑ Door and window hardening

❑ Entry alarms

❑ Community security network

❑ Solar exterior lighting

COMMUNICATIONS

❑ Family Communications Plan (as outlined earlier)

❑ Rechargeable ham/GMRS radios

❑ Cell phone chargers/battery banks

COMMUNITY

❑ Neighbor network established

❑ List of sharable resources/skills

❑ Neighborhood Communications Plan

EVACUATION

❑ Evacuation plan completed

❑ Bug out bag

❑ Bug out vehicle/transportation

❑ Vehicle survival kit

❑ Bug out location options

❑ Bug out routes established

❑ Backup fuel storage (gasoline/diesel)

The idea of becoming self-sufficient in this day and age seems overwhelming. It often makes people think they need more technology, more gadgets, more fancy equipment, and more money. While this is one route to go, I would argue that the opposite is the better option. One hundred and fifty years ago, nearly every household in rural America was self-sufficient. None of them had solar panels, battery backups, refrigerators, dehydrators, freeze dryers, and dozens of other modern devices and appliances. Most of them didn't have vehicles, fancy firearms, electricity, or even running water.

The easier route to self-sufficiency is not to make life more complicated but to simplify. Winding back the clock to configure a system that can operate without (or with very little) electricity can be the most efficient path to self-reliance.

The truth, however, is that self-sufficiency starts in the brain. It's most likely that if you're reading this, you already have a self-sufficient mindset. But what if you don't? What if developing a self-sufficient mindset needs to become your first step toward a more self-sufficient lifestyle? The good news is that this is a skill set and mentality that can be developed.

Building a Self-Sufficient Mindset

The key to growing in any area of life is to intentionally challenge yourself in that area. Self-sufficient thinking is no exception. Start by making a habit of doing things you would normally hire or ask other people to do for you.

This includes things like fixing the toilet; growing vegetables; harvesting and purifying water; dispatching, processing, and cooking an animal for food; and using handheld radios instead of cell phones to communicate with family and community team members. Every time you do something out of your comfort zone, it not only hones a skill set but also builds confidence, and confidence is critical to self-sufficiency.

Making your own choices is also an exercise in self-sufficiency. If you regularly rely on the decisions of government, the media, or others to run your life, then it will be difficult to make your own decisions in the midst of a crisis. Self-sufficient people don't look to others for permission or approval to make decisions about their lives. Become aware of where you are on this spectrum and work to think more independently. Depending on your circumstances, this may prove difficult, but it will boost your self-esteem and decrease your dependency on other people or organizations.

When it comes to your family, create an environment of self-sufficiency. Become a leader who encourages your loved ones to tackle hard problems, find solutions, think independently, and be proactive. Confront entitled mentalities and habits and replace them with personal responsibility and positive reinforcement.

Preparing for When Self-Sufficiency Falls Short

Regardless of how much you plan and prepare both physically and mentally, some disasters require evacuation from home base. While this is certainly not ideal, it is a part of living in an unpredictable world. Wildfires, floods, hurricanes, invasions, acts of terror, and many other events can make staying at home more dangerous than leaving for a safer destination. Because of this, plans for evacuation must be made. One of the first aspects of evacuating is choosing a set of predetermined destinations. Part 3 will discuss what this may look like for you and your family.

PART 3

GO

If it becomes too dangerous to stay at home, evacuation may be necessary. In some instances, it is the only option. Part 3 of this book deals with the harsh reality of leaving your home and everything you've put in place to shelter there. Evacuation is the act of heading for a safer destination.

There are three primary aspects to safely and efficiently evacuating. These include:

- Where to go
- What to take
- How to get there

Advance preparation is critical to making cool and calm decisions during a disaster evacuation. If you've already planned what you're taking with you, where you're going, and how you're getting there, you've got 90 percent of your bases covered. Instead of the frenzy of chaos fueled by panic and fear in the midst of a crisis, evacuation becomes the methodical step-by-step execution of a predetermined plan. It is measurably safer and more effective than making decisions in the moment.

The next three chapters will provide you with the knowledge and corresponding action steps to creating an organized and comprehensive evacuation plan to drastically improve the odds of you and your family getting to a safer destination if staying at home is no longer an option.

CHAPTER 12

WHERE TO GO

While many local and federal disaster recovery organizations such as FEMA have plans for establishing group shelters for evacuees during disasters, this option should not be a part of your evacuation plan. In addition, planning to evacuate to a campground, hotel, or any other lodging option available to the general public is not a plan. All of these places will be congested and overrun with people who are scared, frustrated, injured, and desperate. During a time when first responders are already spread thin, this is not ideal for the safety of your family.

This chapter will focus on choosing a set of strategic evacuation locations. These are different from and in addition to the family meeting places discussed in Chapter 8's Family Communications Plan. Meeting places are predetermined local spots to meet your family if communication is interrupted. Evacuation destinations (also called bug out locations) are the places you will travel to together in the event of an evacuation from home base.

Evacuation Checklist: Before You Go

Before we discuss destination options, following is a broad evacuation checklist for you to use in the event that you do have to evacuate. Evacuations from some disasters have specific actions to consider. These are detailed in Part 4.

- Secure the 8 Ps of Evacuation (Chapter 13 will discuss in more detail):
  - **P**eople
  - **P**ersonal needs (detailed in Chapter 13, under *bug out bag*)
  - **P**rescriptions/First aid kit (detailed in Chapter 9)
  - **P**apers
  - **P**riceless items
  - **P**ets
  - **P**hone/Communications kit (detailed in Chapter 13)
  - **P**ayment (includes multiple methods such as credit cards, checks, and cash)
- Print out Family Communications Plan with complete out-of-town contact information.
- Fill up gas tank with fuel storage (if applicable).
- Turn off propane/natural gas utilities at main valve.
- Turn off water at main valve.
- Turn off electricity at main breaker.
- Drain hot water heater and pipes (in cold weather).
- Flush all toilets to remove water from tank. Put 3 cups antifreeze in tank and in bowl of toilet to prevent water in trap from freezing.
- Put 1 cup antifreeze in all sink, tub, and shower drains to prevent water from freezing and breaking trap.
- Unplug appliances to prevent fire hazards during potential power surges.
- Plug all toilets and drains if a flood is expected to prevent sewage from backflowing into your home.
- Lock all windows and doors.
- Close all blinds.
- Notify your evacuation destination of your departure.

The Importance of Paper Maps

While designing your family evacuation plan, purchase backup paper maps that cover all your chosen destinations. This is a critical detail that many people in the new digital world will overlook. If cellular or GPS services would be unavailable or otherwise fail, it is crucial to be able to reference a paper map. This is true even if you have the route to your destination memorized. One bridge closure, traffic jam, flooded road, or clogged freeway could change your route in an instant. Being able to quickly reroute offline could mean the difference between getting to your destination or being stuck in chaos. These maps can be kept in your 72-hour disaster survival kit (detailed in Chapter 13) for easy reference.

Three Types of Destinations

I used to think having one evacuation destination was sufficient, but I no longer feel that way. I've studied too many instances where either people couldn't get to their intended destination or a disaster was so large it encompassed their predetermined destination. Because of this, I now recommend having a list of three different evacuation ideas. One should be 1–2 hours away, one should be 3–5 hours away, and one should be several states away. Having a few options is always wise. You can always prioritize one of them as your ideal option, but at least you'll still have two backups if something prevents you from evacuating to your ideal spot. But what makes an ideal evacuation destination?

First of all, there are no right or wrong answers to this question. Everyone's circumstances, tastes, budgets, and preferences are different, and all of these affect where you may want to evacuate. However, following is a list of items that are important enough to consider:

- **Population:** Arguments can be made that it is advantageous to get away from people during a large-scale disaster. On the flip side, remote areas are farther from modern resources and conveniences. I do believe that one of your three options should be remote.

- **Distance:** At least one of your evacuation destinations should be within a three-day walk. That is roughly 80–100 miles for most people. If you must abandon your vehicle or other mode of transportation, walking may be your only option.
- **Resources:** Are there resources available at the destination? These include heat, power, food, water, medicine, tools, cooking supplies, and more. I've spoken to many people whose plan is to hike into a national forest somewhere and live off the land. This is naive and unrealistic for 99.9 percent of the population. The fewer resources at the destination, the more plans you will need to make in advance and the more supplies you will need to bring with you.
- **Price:** Is there a cost to choosing a certain destination? If so, does it make sense financially for you?

With these items under consideration, next you will find a list of the most common evacuation locations. None of them are perfect because all disasters are different.

Destination Considerations

As mentioned already, it's important to establish three evacuation destinations outside your general area. One should be 1–2 hours away, one should be 3–5 hours away, and one should be several states away. As you begin to build your own list, here are some of the most common destinations to consider.

RELATIVE'S HOUSE

A close relative is at the top of the list when it comes to evacuation destinations. It's important to discuss your plans with them in advance and notify them of your evacuation as soon as possible so they can plan. You may also be able to negotiate keeping some supplies on location, such as long-term food storage and personal items.

FRIEND'S HOUSE

Like with a relative, it's important to discuss your plans with a friend in advance and notify them of your evacuation as soon as possible so they can prepare.

SECOND HOME/SURVIVAL RETREAT

If your circumstances allow for it, a second home could be an outstanding evacuation destination. It can be stocked in advance with long-term food storage and other items you might need for short-term or even long-term survival. This destination could range from a vacation home to an intentional and fully stocked survival retreat. Some of my customers have purchased a second home specifically as an evacuation destination.

VACATION CONDO

I have a friend who purchased a condo at one of his favorite places to vacation in Florida. He and his family use it several times a year, and he plans on using it as an evacuation option in the event of a large-scale disaster where he lives in Tennessee. He rents it out the rest of the year, and it is an income stream for him and his family.

PRIVATE LAND

If seclusion is your goal, private land in a remote location is an option to consider. If driving an RV or pulling a camper is part of your plan, just having a safe place to call home where you won't get hassled might be appealing. Be sure to consider resources such as food, power, and water once you arrive. It may be wise to set up these utilities in advance.

SURVIVAL BUNKER

While these can be costly, survival bunkers are a big business these days. There are those who bury a bunker in the backyard and those who bury a bunker on a remote plot of land several states away from where they reside full-time. Neither is right or wrong, just different ways of thinking.

MOBILE RV OR CAMPER

There is certainly an appeal to having everything you need in a mobile self-sufficient camper. The cons are that it relies on fuel and you will need a place to park it. And, if evacuation on foot is required, you'll have to abandon your backup plan for living out of the RV.

BOAT

I have several friends whose evacuation destination is a boat with living quarters. One friend's plan is to haul the boat and evacuate with his family to the coast. Another friend has his boat permanently stored near the coast for a quick getaway. Each has made plans to live on the boat with his family for weeks at a time in the event of a large-scale emergency.

ANOTHER COUNTRY

This may sound extreme, but many people have sought citizenship in other countries for the ultimate evacuation if a nationwide event happens. This clearly requires many months or even years of planning but is an option nonetheless.

PUBLIC SHELTERS

While a last resort, it is wise to know the plans and locations of public shelters in case of a disaster in your community or region. You can obtain this information by contacting the emergency management department of your local community or the local Community Emergency Response Team (CERT). If your area doesn't have either one, try contacting the next largest community. A web search for "emergency management + [your community's name]" should give you a place to start. Public shelters, however, are not ideal. In certain circumstances, they can even be dangerous. The stories that came from the public shelters during Hurricane Katrina were horrific to say the least. Make plans so that you can avoid them if possible.

CHAPTER 13

WHAT TO TAKE

By far, most disaster evacuations happen with little to no warning. In addition, many evacuation events such as a flood, wildfire, or hurricane can completely destroy your home and everything in it. This is why knowing exactly what you plan to do and exactly what you plan to take with you is so important. Such planning takes time, and you can't possibly make all the right decisions in the midst of a sudden and unexpected large-scale disaster. It is imperative to do the work before an event. At the top of the list is knowing exactly what you plan to take with you and readying those things for a quick and efficient evacuation.

The 8 Ps of Evacuation

For years, I've taught the 8 Ps of evacuation. These are:

- People
- Personal needs
- Prescriptions/First aid kit
- Papers
- Priceless items
- Pets
- Phone/Communications kit
- Payment (includes multiple methods such as credit cards, checks, and cash)

While every household is different, if you have made plans to include these items, then you'll be well on your way to a quick and efficient evacuation. In this chapter, I will break down the 8 Ps into smaller, more manageable sections. You may have some of them prepared already. Others will take an investment of time, money, and effort. Let's start with the most important category of all: people.

People

Obviously, you want to make sure to evacuate with all your loved ones. This category is less about stating the obvious and more about reminding you that each person has specific needs, and some of those may not be so obvious.

As you review the following categories, keep those with special requirements in mind. Children, seniors, and people with disabilities will need items that you may not. For example, packing diapers and baby formula in your 72-hour disaster survival kit (discussed next) is easy to overlook. Or making sure Grandma has her walker or wheelchair is an easy oversight. If the people you look after and care for need something specific on a regular basis, these items or some version of them will likely need to come with you and should be considered in every category that follows.

Personal Needs

The personal needs category includes your 72-hour disaster survival kit, also called a bug out bag. That's why this is by far the most extensive of all the 8 P categories. A bug out bag is a disaster survival kit prepared in advance to get you and your family through 72 hours of independent survival. It is a backpack that contains all the tools, gear, food, water, medicine, clothing, shelter, hygiene, cooking, fire-starting, and survival products you need to get your family from ground zero to your evacuation location. Each capable individual in the family will likely need their own bug out bag, and children should only carry lightweight necessities.

It is important to note that a bug out bag is designed not only to be portable and ready to grab at a moment's notice but also to be carried on foot

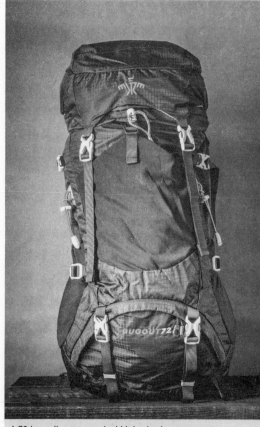

A 72-hour disaster survival kit is also known as a bug out bag. Photo credit: Anthony at AnthonyAwaken.com

in the event vehicle travel isn't possible. For this reason, I recommend choosing a comfortable hiking or camping backpack as your bug out bag. Inside will be the bare minimum of supplies you need to get from point A to point B.

Following is a list of items to consider including in your bug out bag, broken down by survival category:

Shelter
- Backpacking tent large enough to fit all the people you plan to take with you

- Weather-appropriate sleeping bags
- Sleeping pads
- Fresh change of T-shirt, underwear, and socks
- Fresh change of clothing (if space allows)
- Weather-appropriate shoes/boots (to be worn during evacuation)
- Rain gear/poncho
- Emergency survival blanket

Water

- 1-liter metal canteen filled with fresh drinking water (you can boil and purify more)
- Sawyer Products mini (or similar) camping water filter (for filtering water on the go)
- One or two collapsible plastic water containers
- Sillcock key (for accessing commercial water spigots)

Fire

- Ferro rod fire starter
- Disposable lighter
- Fire tinder

Food

- Open-and-eat meals such as tuna packs, Spam, power bars, beef jerky, and dried snacks (open-and-eat meals do not require stopping to prepare food and eliminate the need for a stove)
- Small camp stove along with freeze-dried camping meals (as an alternative to open-and-eat meals)
- Utensils
- Serving bowls (if applicable)

First Aid

- First aid kit (see Chapter 9)
- Prescription medication

Hygiene
- Toilet paper and/or wet wipes
- Personal hygiene products
- Small bar of soap in resealable bag
- Toothbrush and toothpaste

Tools
- Fixed-blade knife
- Multi-tool with pliers
- Small folding saw
- Rechargeable headlamp
- Signal whistle

Self-Defense
- Personal firearm
- Nonlethal self-defense item such as pepper spray

Miscellaneous
- Paper maps to evacuation destination
- Permanent marker
- Duct tape
- Entertainment items such as an easily portable game or a pack of cards (these are great for kids)
- Cash (discussed in detail later in this chapter)
- Important documents (discussed in detail later in this chapter)

All of these items should be stored in one or multiple backpacks. Hike several miles wearing your fully loaded pack to make sure it is comfortable and realistic. Backpacks with adjustable shoulder straps and waist belts are best and can be found in the camping section at most outdoor retailers. A good average size is 40–45 liters, and I have provided links to several options for you, along with links to many of my favorite bug out bag items, at the online resource page for this book: CreekStewart.com/disasterready.

Prescriptions/First Aid Kit

You have several options when it comes to a first aid kit for your bug out bag. You can create a smaller, lighter-weight version of the one described in Chapter 9, or you can plan on taking your at-home first aid kit with you by packing it in a second bug out bag carried by another family member. Other family members should have more room in their packs because it isn't necessary for everyone to carry duplicates of items such as tools, a tent, water filter, or camp stove, for example.

For me and my family of four, I have created a smaller, bug out bag–specific first aid kit. I plan on also evacuating with my larger at-home first aid kit with the understanding that I may have to leave it behind in the vehicle if for some reason we would need to walk. Ideally, that kit makes it to our evacuation destination, but I can live without it if necessary.

In addition to the medical supplies already discussed, it is critical to review what medications must be taken with you during evacuation. This is where that thirty-day backup supply of medications is really important, especially for those whose life and health depend on daily medication. These medications can be added to a bug out bag at the last minute or kept with it at all times and changed out during maintenance cycles. It's a good idea to replace all consumables in your bug out bag every six months or at their respective expiration dates.

Papers

There are many reasons to keep important papers and documentation organized in a safe place and ready to grab at a moment's notice. Evacuation is certainly one of those. Replacing important documents can be expensive, time-consuming, and frustrating. Having these documents on hand is also very important when dealing with authorities during a disaster and/or putting your life back together after a disaster. Bottom line, there is a long list of important documents that would make your life a lot easier if you didn't lose them during a disaster. These include:

- Driver's license
- Passport

- Birth certificate
- Marriage certificate
- Medical records
- Bank accounts
- Credit card information
- Insurance policies
- Deed
- Lease
- Utility bills and company information
- Tax records (business, personal, property)
- Vaccination records

Some of these documents can be stored in paper form inside a waterproof resealable bag. Some of them can also be stored on a thumb drive for access later. During normal times, they can reside in a fireproof safe inside the home. In the event of an evacuation, they can be quickly placed in bug out bags for safe keeping during travel.

Priceless Items

If there is a chance your home will be destroyed, it may be wise to have a storage tote on hand to bring some of your priceless items with you. Looting and vandalism often come in the wake of a disaster as well. The caveat to taking items with you is that if you are forced to travel on foot, you may have to leave items behind in your vehicle. It can be a gamble either way and will have to be a personal decision.

Priceless items are different for everyone. They can include photos, computer hard drives, laptops, firearms, special gifts, heirlooms, jewelry, or anything else that is considered irreplaceable. Consider making a list of these items so that you can gather them quickly in the event of an evacuation.

Pets

If you plan on your pets coming with you, they will need items as well. Ideally these items are organized in advance so that loading them in the car is quick, stress-free, and easy. Here is a checklist of pet-related needs to consider:

- Food (72 hours' worth)
- Water
- Medicines
- Shot/vaccination records (could be required at checkpoints or shelters)
- Collar with identification tag
- Leash
- Carrier/travel crate
- Waste bags
- Muzzle
- Microchip information
- Portable food/water bowls

Phone/Communications Kit

While communications was covered at length in Chapter 8, that was primarily for a shelter-in-place scenario. It is important to also consider evacuating with a small communications kit to make sure you can keep in touch with loved ones who are with you or at your evacuation destination.

Items in this kit would also allow you to receive emergency updates en route. These items can easily be incorporated into your bug out bag, or they can be stowed in a separate bag or kit that goes into the vehicle with you. Following is a checklist of items to consider adding to your mobile communications kit:

- Cell phone
- Cell phone charger (car)
- Cell phone charger (home)
- Portable backup battery bank (I use one from the company Anker that will charge my cell phone seven times; it will also charge my other USB-rechargeable devices such as my headlamp, GMRS radios, and ham radios)

A mobile communications kit allows you to receive emergency updates en route to your evacuation destination.

- Small portable solar charger (the one I use is from GoalZero)
- GMRS/ham radios
- Satellite phone (if applicable)
- Dedicated NOAA Weather Radio or NOAA-compatible two-way radios (to receive emergency and weather-related updates in your area)
- Printed copy of your Family Communications Plan with out-of-town contact information
- Waterproof dry bags (for transport and storage of all mentioned items)

Payment

Evacuating with multiple forms of payment is smart. It's very possible that grid failures will prevent digital or credit card payments. Having printed checks, cash in various denominations, and even barter items can be extremely advantageous. Cash can be kept in a hidden undergarment waist belt like travelers use. I recommend having a minimum of several hundred dollars on hand if your budget allows. The cash should be in various denominations. I'll never forget a conversation I had with evacuees from Hurricane Katrina in Houston, Texas. They couldn't get gas, book a room, or buy groceries because all forms of digital payment were temporarily down. They ended up in a church shelter, dependent on donations and handouts until they could access their money.

Extending Your Knowledge

In this chapter I've included a lot of information about items to consider taking with you during an evacuation. If you feel you need more in-depth information and training about building a 72-hour disaster survival kit, I would recommend picking up a copy of my book *Build the Perfect Bug Out Bag*. In this book I go into much more detail and also teach many skills about building a disaster survival kit. You can find it anywhere books are sold or at the link I've provided at the online resource page for this book: CreekStewart.com/disasterready.

As I've mentioned previously, you may be forced to leave your belongings twice: once when evacuating

My book *Build the Perfect Bug Out Bag* teaches how to build a 72-hour disaster survival kit. Photo credit: Anthony at AnthonyAwaken.com

your home and then again if travel by vehicle becomes impossible. A few months ago, I received an email from a customer who used my book *Build the Perfect Bug Out Bag* to create their disaster survival kit. They lived in Colorado and had to evacuate their home due to a raging wildfire. They had only a few hours' notice. While evacuating in their vehicle, traffic became jammed and they were forced to park their vehicle on the side of the road and walk over 30 miles to a safer destination. They lived out of their bug out bags for two full days until a relative was able to pick them up and take them to a nearby town. Thankfully, evacuating on foot is rare. In the next chapter, we'll discuss the topic of transportation during a disaster evacuation.

CHAPTER 14

HOW TO GET THERE

In a disaster, your transportation strategy can be just as important as your decision to leave. This chapter will help you outline a comprehensive plan for getting from point A to point B as safely and efficiently as possible.

We've already discussed the importance of having paper maps marked with contingency routes to your array of evacuation destinations. But there are many other things to consider when it comes to the traveling portion of evacuation. In this chapter, I'll expound on different options for vehicular transportation (public and private), vehicle emergency kits, and some possibilities to consider if you have to travel on foot. By the end, you'll have a clear understanding of gaps in your evacuation transportation plan that may need to be addressed.

A hitch-mounted cargo basket can be installed with basic tools on most models of vehicles.

Evacuation Vehicle

For most people, their daily driving vehicle will be their evacuation vehicle. Some people may have a vehicle outfitted especially for such circumstances. That's nice but not necessary. Besides being in good working order, attributes to consider when choosing an evacuation vehicle include the following:

CARGO STORAGE

The 8 Ps of evacuation (see Chapter 13) can take up a lot of space. A small vehicle can limit your ability to take what you want with you. Overnighting in a small vehicle is also very uncomfortable. If a smaller vehicle is your only option, consider adding a roof rack or other roof storage to gain cargo space. Another option is a hitch-mounted cargo basket, but this requires your vehicle to have a tow hitch receiver. These cost a few hundred dollars and can be installed with basic tools on most models of vehicles.

DISTANCE

The ability to travel to one or two of your evacuation destinations on one tank of gas or one battery charge is very important. Getting gas or recharging will likely be out of the question. In almost every large-scale evacuation I have studied, gas stations were either incredibly backed up, not open, or out of gas altogether. This highlights the importance of having enough fuel storage at home to top off your gas tank at any given moment in the event of a sudden evacuation. Exterior mounted fuel tanks, such as military-style jerricans, are another option if that is possible on your vehicle. Fuel cans can also be mounted on hitch racks or roof cargo baskets.

OFF-ROAD CAPABILITY

Whether driving on road shoulders, taking roads less traveled, or traversing snow and ice, off-road-capable vehicles give you more options when it comes to evacuation. There are countless instances during a large-scale evacuation to need a four-wheel-drive vehicle capable of driving off the paved path—or over debris, snow, or mud that has accumulated on the road.

Preparing Your Vehicle for Evacuation

In addition to the vehicle itself, it is critical to have a well-thought-out vehicle emergency kit. Because you'll have most of your survival items packed in bug out bags, this kit contains mainly vehicle-specific items that will be used for maintenance, repair, and getting out of trouble. Following is a sample checklist of items to include in a vehicle emergency kit. Most of these items can be neatly stored in a durable tote in the trunk.

- Full-sized spare tire
- Full-sized floor jack (most jacks that come with cars are very hard to use)
- Full-sized tire iron
- Tire plug kit with reamer, plug tool, and one-dozen plugs

- DC tire pump
- 50-foot tow rope
- Tire sealant
- Traction aids (chains, folding treads)
- Jumper cables
- Basic tool kit with wrenches, screwdrivers, ratchet set, duct tape, hammer, etc.
- Small fire extinguisher
- Work gloves
- Rechargeable flashing roadside triangle
- Neon reflective vest
- Important documents (in glove box) that include vehicle manual, vehicle registration, and proof of insurance
- Extra antifreeze, oil, and window washer fluid
- Chainsaw if you have room (for downed trees)

You'll use items stored in a vehicle emergency kit for maintenance, repair, and getting out of trouble.

Alternative Transportation

If a sudden evacuation from a large city such as Los Angeles, Chicago, New York, or even a much smaller city is ordered, traveling by vehicle will be impossible. History tells us that roadways will be gridlocked with bumper-to-bumper traffic, broken-down vehicles, vehicles that have run out of gas or battery power, and crashes. In these instances of mass exodus, your only options will be to travel on foot or utilize an alternate form of transportation.

It is my opinion that an e-bike is the best option. It offers assisted power and operates as a normal pedal bike. Small bike trailers can be hauled, and many e-bikes have cargo racks and child seat options. Normal pedal bikes also allow you to weave in and out of gridlocked traffic. Both types of bikes can be roof mounted or hitch mounted to travel with your vehicle if evacuation is necessary.

A pull-behind trailer with a dirt bike, motorcycle, or ATV also provides a backup solution in the event you have to abandon a full-sized vehicle.

Even small electric scooters can travel anywhere from 20 to 100 miles depending on the model. These could be used and abandoned when the battery fails. With an average speed of 10 mph, and as a quick and easy way to travel 20-plus miles during a critical evacuation time period, this kind of scooter could justify its cost.

Navigating Road Closures and Obstacles

The number one way to mitigate road closures, gridlocked traffic, and obstacles is to plan ahead and evacuate as early as possible. It is human nature to wait until the last minute, but if you do the work now and can be ready to leave within a few minutes of a large-scale crisis, you can avoid the bulk of problems many will encounter on the road.

Planning backup routes can also help navigate around obstacles. Knowing these options in advance can help you make quick, educated decisions while on the move. Most people will be at the mercy of what their GPS is telling them. And the GPS will be telling all of them the same thing. Taking the road less traveled could be your best option.

Having multiple evacuation destinations will also give you the option to be flexible. If one direction is blocked, a destination in the opposite direction could be your only choice. Knowing these options in advance and having a paper map are critical.

Public Transportation

If you or someone you love relies on public transportation, then evacuation options, if available, can be extremely limited. But this is a reality for some people. The key is to ask the authority in charge of public transportation in your community about their evacuation policies in advance of an event. As an example, the Jacksonville Transportation Authority in Jacksonville, Florida, offers evacuation services in the event of a hurricane, but preregistration is required and residents needing this service must register every year. In addition, public transportation only provides services to public shelters, and you are not able to choose which shelter you are delivered to.

Special Considerations for Traveling on Foot

You should always be prepared to travel on foot, even if you're evacuating by vehicle. There are numerous scenarios that may require abandoning a vehicle in order to keep moving away from a disaster.

72-HOUR BACKPACK (BUG OUT BAG)

It is important that your bug out bag be a backpack. A backpack allows you to hike comfortably while carrying a significant amount of gear. It also keeps your hands free for carrying other items and helping other people in your evacuation party. Testing your pack in advance is essential to make sure it's comfortable and practical.

CARTS, STROLLERS, WAGONS, WHEELCHAIRS, AND TRAILERS

Traveling with children, people with disabilities, or older adults presents specific challenges when going by foot. In these instances, you'll need to consider options for potentially pushing or pulling them along for the ride. Whether on foot or by bike, there are numerous workable options to consider.

Even if an older member of your family doesn't use a wheelchair, it may be a wise investment for evacuation purposes. Make sure it is compact enough to be brought along in your evacuation vehicle. Motorized wheelchairs can present problems if recharging isn't an option due to grid failure.

For children, wagons and strollers are excellent options. Lightweight foldable wagons can be purchased for under $50 and present a compact solution for toting children if they get tired. Large, wheeled jogging strollers are an incredible option as these are designed for jogging on trails and are very easy to push.

Pull-behind bicycle trailers are also an amazing option to consider. Even if you aren't using a bicycle, these trailers can be rigged to a harness or belt or simply held by hand. They have large tires and ample cargo space and travel very well even on bumpy terrain.

Carts, wagons, and trailers aren't just for people. They can be used to carry other items from the 8 P categories, including but not limited to extra gear, bug out bags, shelter items, and more. Along with *Facebook Marketplace*, thrift stores are a great place to find random carts and trailers that could be used for such a purpose.

The Multi-Purpose Cart from Mighty Max Cart (https://mightymaxcart.com) is an excellent option for toting gear across various terrain conditions.

One cart that I really like is the American-made Multi-Purpose Cart from MightyMaxCart.com. It is lightweight, holds a heavy load, and has wide wheels that don't bog down in mud, gravel, or grass.

My family and I use the Mighty Max Cart Multi-Purpose Cart to haul gear and my five-year-old daughter on our practice bug out drill.

Regardless of whether you're in a vehicle or on foot, effective transportation is key to successfully navigating out of danger zones. In the next part, we will look at specific disaster and emergency scenarios. I'll be outlining the specific threats for each disaster, along with strategies for staying home or evacuating, including how transportation strategies may vary depending on the type of emergency.

PART 4

DISASTERS AND EMERGENCY SITUATIONS

There are a number of disasters that could happen at any given moment. History is an amazing teacher, and we can learn a great deal by studying what has already happened. While every single disaster is unique, previous events provide us with concrete clues as to the best preparations to make and actions to take.

In the following sections, I will break down twenty-three different disasters and emergencies, based on previous data, to help provide you with a decision-making action plan either before or in the midst of the crisis. For each scenario, I supply the following:

- Overview of the disaster, detailing the most common threats

- Immediate action steps
- Factors supporting a decision to stay
- Checklist for safe and effective staying
- Factors supporting a decision to evacuate
- Checklist for safe and effective evacuation

This part of the book is your ultimate disaster guide for mitigating and navigating the world's most likely cataclysmic events. It can be a tool for advance study to better prepare your existing strategies, or it can be a reference manual in the midst of a crisis to facilitate you in making calm and educated decisions.

ACTIVE SHOOTER

An active shooter is attempting to kill people around them. They are in possession of a firearm and shooting randomly. The weapon may intimidate bystanders and prevent first responders or law enforcement from approaching. Other weapons used include knives, blunt objects, and explosives. Although an active shooter incident usually lasts only 15 minutes, it is extremely dangerous. You need to remain calm and respond quickly.

Active shooters typically target crowded, busy places like schools and shopping centers. They are often fueled by rage or hatred and can be unpredictable. Active shooters are sometimes suicidal, have nothing to lose, and show no mercy to men, women, or children.

Having situational awareness could save you. This is simply being aware and taking stock of your surroundings in every environment. Following are three examples of situational awareness in an active shooter scenario:

- Locate any available exits including emergency exits or windows.
- Locate large objects that could become cover, including walls, kiosks, cars, trees, or statues.
- Observe people around you, especially anyone who does not seem to fit in. Active shooters sometimes dress in army-style clothing or clothing inappropriate for the weather, such as heavy clothing in midsummer. They may carry large duffel-style bags.

Immediate Action

Remember that law enforcement won't arrive immediately. It's imperative to keep a cool head, as you don't want to run into the shooter's line of fire. There are three actions you can take: run, hide, or fight. The first two are preferable.

Survival Decisions: GO

Factors supporting fleeing during an active shooter scenario include:

- The shooter is some distance away, and there is an opportunity to flee.

✓ Checklist for Safe and Effective Evacuation

- ❑ Run the minute you hear gunshots or even a noise you think might be gunshots.
- ❑ Don't retrieve your belongings, shopping bags, or anything else besides your loved ones.
- ❑ Move between places of cover. Cover includes any kind of structure or fixture including walls, cars, benches, and landscaping pots.
- ❑ Move toward an exit.
- ❑ If you are in proximity to the shooter and you need to cross an area with no cover, wait for a pause in gunfire, as the shooter might be reloading. Run between locations as fast as possible.
- ❑ If you encounter law enforcement, show them your hands and tell them where you last saw the shooter.
- ❑ Check your party for injuries.
- ❑ Dial 911 as soon as you are safe, just in case no one has called yet.

Survival Decisions: STAY

Factors supporting hiding during an active shooter include:

- The shooter is too close for you to leave.
- There is someone in your party with mobility issues.

✓ Checklist for Safe and Effective Hiding

❏ A room with thick walls and few or no windows is best.

❏ Lock the doors and/or barricade them with any available furniture or obstacles.

❏ Turn off the lights and silence phones and other devices.

❏ Close windows and blinds so that you cannot be seen from outside.

❏ If a room is not available, hide in the darkest, most remote area possible, preferably behind or under cover. Silence all phones and devices.

❏ If you are outside, hide behind a wall, large tree, or building. If you cannot see the shooter, the shooter cannot see you.

❏ Stay quiet and out of sight until things have calmed down.

❏ Stay low to the ground.

Survival Decisions: FIGHT BACK

Factors supporting fighting back during an active shooter include:

• You cannot run or hide.
• You have specialized training and/or equipment to effectively fight back (e.g., firearms training).

✓ Checklist for Safe and Effective Fighting

❏ If you are with others, spread out so that the shooter has multiple targets.

❏ Throw nearby objects, such as chairs or fire extinguishers, at the shooter to incapacitate them and disrupt their actions.

❏ Work together with others whenever possible.

❏ If using a firearm, be aware of others who may be in front of or behind the shooter.

❏ When possible, approach the shooter from behind while they are distracted.

❏ Disable, disarm, and dial 911.

❏ You may not be able to leave until instructed by law enforcement.

AVALANCHE

An avalanche occurs when snow and ice plunge rapidly down a slope. When an avalanche stops, the snow rapidly solidifies, making it difficult for people trapped in the avalanche to breathe or escape. Flooding may occur afterward, which could reroute rivers and isolate mountain towns and resorts.

Immediate Action

Avalanches move at around 60–80 mph and occur mainly from December to April. If you are caught in an avalanche, you can improve your chances of survival by immediately doing the following depending on your circumstances:

- If you have triggered the avalanche, move quickly uphill, getting above the fracture line as fast as possible.
- Move to the side of the avalanche as quickly as you can, as it is most dangerous in the center, where there is the most snow.
- Get rid of heavy equipment and large packs but try to keep lifesaving items such as a two-way radio, probe, or snow shovel.
- If you can, try to anchor yourself to a large tree or boulder.
- If hit by an avalanche, try to "swim" across the surface in an uphill direction as best you can.
- If buried, quickly shoot an arm up above your head so that your hand appears above the snow and rescuers can find you. If you aren't sure where the surface is, spit out some saliva, as gravity will pull it downward.
- Immediately after the avalanche stops, take action to give yourself some breathing room before the snow begins the process of settling. Dig an air pocket around your nose and mouth so that you can breathe. The snow will rapidly set hard (called sintering), so you need to do this as quickly as possible. It will give you some extra critical minutes of breathing time. Try not to panic, as you will breathe faster.
- If you are close to the surface, you might be able to dig yourself out, but this isn't usually possible. Stay quiet and still and wait. If you used an

avalanche beacon and probe, your rescuers will find them on the surface, and they may see your hand and arm if you managed to get them out of the snow.

The best strategy is to avoid avalanches altogether. Avalanches happen suddenly, and there's minimal time to prepare. However, you can minimize your exposure by:

- Keeping in touch with local avalanche authorities and know your local avalanche risk.
- Avoiding high-risk areas and slopes steeper than 90 degrees.
- Noticing cracking, collapsing snow, or strange noises, as these could indicate instability.
- Wearing a helmet to reduce head injuries and create air pockets.
- Traveling with a partner so that you can look after one another.
- Wearing brightly colored clothes to increase your visibility.

Survival Decisions: STAY

It is important to note that if your home is located in the path of a potential avalanche, it is always recommended to evacuate if possible.

Factors supporting staying in place during an avalanche include:

- Authorities have not issued an evacuation order.
- Your home is not in the path or near the path of a potential avalanche.
- Your home is well equipped to deal with cold temperatures and power outages.
- You have backup heat sources in place.
- You've made advance preparations to shelter in place without access to food, water, power, and medical facilities for an undetermined period of time.
- Evacuation routes are blocked.
- Travel has become dangerous due to heavy snow or ice.

✓ Checklist for Safe and Effective Staying

- ❏ Remain in ground-floor rooms or the basement until the authorities give the all clear.
- ❏ Monitor NOAA Weather Radio and news broadcasts for emergency information.
- ❏ Keep pets indoors.
- ❏ When you can go out, check that your gas furnace vent is not blocked by snow. This could cause carbon monoxide to backflow into the home.
- ❏ Be cautious using heaters and fireplaces. Keep all flammable materials at least 15 feet away.
- ❏ Create and equip a shelter in the basement or lower floor of your home where you can live for several days.
- ❏ Keep snow-clearing tools, flashlights, and replacement batteries in accessible places once the threat begins.
- ❏ Wear an avalanche receiver and probe—the receiver issues a signal indicating where the person is buried, while the probe locates the person for rescuers.
- ❏ Close all windows and doors.
- ❏ Remain in the building.
- ❏ Switch off electrical appliances that are not essential.
- ❏ Gather warm outdoor clothing and sturdy winter boots.
- ❏ Bring out your bug out bag, essential documents, cash, and valuables.
- ❏ Prepare for evacuation just in case.
- ❏ If the power goes out:
  - Move to one central room and cover the windows with blankets and/or window films to maintain heat.
  - Keep refrigerator and freezer doors closed.
  - Monitor medication that needs refrigeration.
  - Disconnect electronics and appliances to avoid damage if there are spikes when power returns.
  - Use backup heat options such as space heaters or a wood stove.

- Dress for cold temperatures with multiple layers of loose-fitting clothing.
- Prepare a group sleeping area to share heat.

Survival Decisions: GO

Factors supporting evacuation during an avalanche include:

- Authorities have issued an evacuation order.
- Your home is located in or near the path of a potential avalanche.
- You have not made advance preparations with food, water, or backup power to live for a few days off the grid.
- Your home or building construction is not conducive to the force of an avalanche.

✔ Checklist for Safe and Effective Evacuation

- ❏ Implement your Family Communications Plan.
- ❏ Implement your evacuation plan; choose a route and destination based on the known avalanche threat.
- ❏ Top off your vehicle's fuel tank with stored fuel.
- ❏ Avalanches can potentially destroy your home. Prepare your evacuation vehicle by packing the 8 Ps of evacuation.
- ❏ Pack extra blankets and bedding material just in case you become stranded in your vehicle.
- ❏ Secure all doors and windows.
- ❏ Wear full winter gear with boots, hat, and face covering.
- ❏ Turn on your headlights.
- ❏ Monitor NOAA Weather Radio and news broadcasts for emergency updates.

❏ Make sure your pickax, snow shovel, flashlight, and extra batteries are on hand.

❏ Stay in your vehicle.

❏ Stop only when you are out of the danger area.

BIOLOGICAL ATTACK

A biological attack occurs when disease-causing viruses, bacteria, fungi (pathogens), or poisonous natural substances (biotoxins) are deliberately released. Also known as bioterrorism, the intention is to harm people, making them sick or killing them to engender fear, disrupt communities, and damage economies. Some pathogens can also transmit diseases.

Biological attacks are more dangerous and insidious than nuclear attacks, as they go undetected until people, animals, or plants develop symptoms. Pinpointing the source of the initial release is often difficult, while identifying the agent requires laboratory testing or tracing infected people back to the first person who developed symptoms. This can be time-consuming.

A biological agent can potentially kill significant numbers of people, depending on how virulent it is, how much is released, how long it takes to identify the pathogen or biotoxin, and how long it takes to treat exposed or infected individuals.

Immediate Action

In the event of a suspected biological attack, you can take these actions to safeguard yourself:

- Follow news reports to learn about the agent used, symptoms of infection, the region affected, and available treatments.
- Establish whether your area has been affected.
- Move away if you suspect that you have encountered a suspicious substance.
- Wear a face mask or protect your nose and mouth by covering them with layers of cotton cloth or clothing.
- Avoid crowds, which may include infected people.
- If you have been exposed, remove your clothing and personal items and bag them. Follow official instructions concerning their disposal. Wash yourself using only soap and water and put on clean clothes. Contact the

authorities for further advice and assistance. Follow their instructions, including quarantining if necessary.

- If you are sick, wear a face mask and limit your contact with others to avoid spreading the disease.
- Symptoms of common illnesses may be similar to those of biological agents, so falling sick doesn't necessarily mean that you have been exposed. Seek medical advice from your doctor or health professional, and practice good hygiene and cleanliness.
- If you are in an area the authorities believe has been targeted by bioterrorists and develop symptoms that appear to align with the agent released, seek medical attention quickly. If the disease is contagious, you may be quarantined. Otherwise, you will simply receive medical treatment.
- Follow the directions of medical professionals and health officials.

Survival Decisions: GO

Evacuation is rarely recommended during biological attacks for several reasons; however, here are factors supporting evacuation during a biological attack:

- Authorities have issued an evacuation order.
- You know the details of where the attack originated so that you can avoid it.
- You are certain you can take a route that avoids exposure.

✓ Checklist for Safe and Effective Evacuation

❑ Implement your Family Communications Plan.

❑ Implement your evacuation plan; choose a route and destination based on the known location of the biological threat.

❑ Top off your vehicle's fuel tank with stored fuel.

❑ Biological threats will not destroy your home. However, you may be away for an undetermined period of time. Prepare your evacuation vehicle by packing the 8 Ps of evacuation.

- Pack additional personal protective gear such as N95 face masks, disinfection wipes and solutions, disposable gloves, garbage bags for storing waste or exposed materials, and extra water for washing and hygiene.
- Monitor NOAA Weather Radio and news broadcasts for emergency updates.
- Stay in your vehicle.
- Stop only when you are out of the danger area.

Survival Decisions: STAY

In the event of a biological agent being released, staying in place is recommended due to the variables at play. If the aerosol plume is widespread and the area it covers too large to enable quick and safe evacuation, then sheltering in place is also preferred.

✓ Checklist for Safe and Effective Staying

- Unless your building is equipped with a HEPA filter capable of filtering out very small particles, it will be necessary to reduce or stop the flow of incoming air while the emergency exists or the contamination plume is passing through the neighborhood.
- Reduce the indoor-outdoor air exchange rate before the plume reaches your building by closing all external doors and windows and turning off fans, air-conditioning, and heaters.
- As soon as the plume has passed, increase the indoor-outdoor air exchange by opening external doors and windows and turning on fans to ventilate the building.
- Sheltering inside a building is only recommended for a maximum of 2 hours, as the protective effect decreases as the incident continues. Buildings release contaminated air gradually, so the amount of contaminants present will eventually exceed those outside.

❏ If you are at home when the emergency is declared, take the following actions:

-   Monitor news broadcasts to receive current information about the emergency.
-   Close all external doors and windows.
-   Switch off air conditioners, fans, and combustion heaters.
-   Close chimney or fireplace dampers.
-   Close air vents or tape them up (for details, see "Chemical or Hazardous Materials Incident," which follows).
-   Enter your safe room, if you have one, making sure all doors and windows are closed and taped shut to prevent contaminants from entering the room.
-   As soon as the plume or threat has passed, open windows and doors, and turn on smoke fans and similar systems to purge your home of any contaminants that may have entered.

CHEMICAL OR HAZARDOUS MATERIALS INCIDENT

A chemical incident happens when a toxic substance that can harm the public and the environment is released accidentally, intentionally, or during a natural disaster. This can happen slowly or gradually, like when a chemical leaks silently into the environment. Examples include:

- Explosion at a chemical production plant or storage facility
- Oil spill
- Chemical contamination of food or water
- Leaks during transportation
- Outbreak of a disease related to chemical exposure
- Deliberate release of chemicals due to terrorism or wars

The level of emergency response depends on the type of contamination and its spread. It is relatively easy to clear a small release that has caused minimal pollution, compared to a terrorist attack that has exposed numerous people and contaminated a wide geographical area.

You can be exposed to a chemical without seeing or smelling anything unusual. Signs of exposure may include skin or eye irritation; burning in the nose, throat, or lungs; breathing difficulties; nausea; or disorientation.

Immediate Actions

If a chemical emergency is declared, you will receive information via radio or television networks, sirens, NOAA Weather Radio, or police and emergency personnel knocking on your door. Stay calm and monitor the news for updates. Avoid calling 911 to leave lines open for first responders and injured people. Follow the instructions of safety officials.

If you are exposed to a hazardous chemical:

- Cover your nose and mouth with cloth, a scarf, or anything you have available.

- If you are outside, move upwind of your current location.
- Go inside and shelter in place, preferably in a windowless room—avoid basements or cellars, as some toxic gasses accumulate at the lowest point in buildings.
- Close windows and doors and turn off air-conditioning and ventilation systems, fans, and furnaces.
- Seal off the room with plastic sheeting and duct tape—you can use towels and trash bags if you don't have plastic sheeting.
- Stay in the shelter until emergency officials give the all clear.

If you might have been contaminated:

- Undress and shower, ideally in the first 10 minutes after exposure, to remove the chemical from your skin and hair.
- If you cannot shower, wipe off as much as you can with a damp cloth.
- Go to the nearest hospital, call the Poison Help line (1-800-222-1222), or visit PoisonHelp.org.

Survival Decisions: GO

If officials tell you to evacuate in the event of a chemical emergency, leave as soon as possible.

✓ Checklist for Safe and Effective Evacuation

- ❏ Implement your Family Communications Plan.
- ❏ Implement your evacuation plan; choose a route and destination based on the known location of the chemical emergency.
- ❏ Top off your vehicle's fuel tank with stored fuel.
- ❏ Chemical emergencies will not destroy your home. However, you may be away for an undetermined period of time. Prepare your evacuation vehicle by packing the 8 Ps of evacuation.
- ❏ Pack additional personal protective gear such as N95 face masks, disinfection wipes and solutions, disposable gloves, garbage bags for storing waste or exposed materials, and extra water for washing and hygiene.

- ❏ Monitor NOAA Weather Radio and news broadcasts for emergency updates.
- ❏ If you have time, seal your home so that contaminants won't enter it. Otherwise, simply close all windows, vents, and fireplace dampers.
- ❏ Turn off appliances except for your refrigerator and freezer.
- ❏ Close and lock your doors and windows.
- ❏ Stay in your vehicle.
- ❏ Stop only when you are out of the danger area.

Survival Decisions: STAY

Shelter-in-place instructions are recommended during chemical emergencies. You will usually need to stay in place for 12 hours at the most.

✓ Checklist for Safe and Effective Staying

- ❏ Find an interior room aboveground in which to shelter, preferably with minimal or no windows.
- ❏ Avoid using elevators, as this may draw in contaminated air.
- ❏ Take out your bug out bag if available.
- ❏ Shut and lock windows and doors and turn off air-conditioning, heaters, and fans. Close and cover all vents.
- ❏ Heavy plastic sheeting, towels, and duct tape can be used to seal your doors and windows in the event of a chemical emergency. Practice doing this beforehand as a drill with your family.
- ❏ If necessary, cover your nose and mouth with a wet cloth. Use N95 face masks if available.
- ❏ Tune in to radio and television stations to keep updated on the status of the emergency.
- ❏ Do not drink tap water, as it may be contaminated.
- ❏ Wait for officials to give you the all clear before going outside.

CRUSHING MOB

A crowd crush happens when a large group of people crowded into one place move off simultaneously, often in response to a real or perceived danger. This can disrupt the pedestrian flow. Stampedes can happen where streets narrow, so crowds funnel into ever smaller places.

If anyone falls, others may fall with them, creating a domino effect. Not knowing what has happened, others might decide to leave, so the crowd heads in one direction, trampling others who are smaller, moving more slowly, or walking counter to the flow. Anxiety and heat increase the chances of people becoming lightheaded or fainting, making them more likely to be crushed. People in stampedes can be squeezed so that they literally can't breathe. If there is an obstruction, those most likely to be injured are those forced against barriers or walls.

Immediate Action

In a crowd faced with danger, panicked people start fleeing. If enough people start running, this may cause mass flight, where a large crowd starts running mindlessly to escape. These situations may be caused by terror attacks, mass shootings, or even certain natural disasters. There is a very real risk that you could fall and be trampled underfoot. If you find yourself in a stampede, do the following:

- If you can't keep up, break away as soon as you can and find a sturdy pillar, large tree, utility pole, or vehicle to shield you from the crowd.
- Stay on your feet.
- Don't fight the crowd and instead go with the flow so that you are less likely to be injured.
- Don't put your purse or backpack on the ground, as obstacles make falls and injuries more likely.
- Breathe normally and don't shout. Conserve your energy.

- Work your way toward the edges of the crowd, as fewer people will be there. Moving diagonally will make it easier for you to reach the edges. During a stampede, there will be lulls in the pushing and shoving. When these happen, you can also move closer to the edges of the crowd.
- To ensure that you can breathe, hold your hands in front of your chest, like a boxer, to maintain enough space for your lungs to expand.
- If you fall, curl into a ball and protect your head and neck with your arms.
- Avoid doorways, hallways, bridges, or other narrow spaces, as the crowd will bottleneck there. Look up and see whether you can escape, by going up a stairway to another level, for example. If you are in the street, turn into a side street or go into a building and allow the mob to move on.

While stampedes often take people by surprise, there are things you can do to improve your situational awareness:

- Attend an event with a companion so that you can take care of one another. Wear bright clothing so that you stand out in the crowd. Avoid wearing long, flowing clothes; scarves; or jewelry that can get caught or tangled. Wear comfortable shoes and make sure the laces are securely tied.
- If the forecast is for rain, be aware that people might stampede, as they seek shelter when the weather worsens.
- Decide where to park ahead of time so that you don't need to rush.
- Have your ID and cell phone with you. Take a water bottle and drink plenty of fluids so that you don't get dizzy or lightheaded.
- When you enter a venue or event arena, note possible exits, including windows, fire exits, barriers, and fences. These could provide escape routes from a mindless crowd. Note the location of the first aid and security stations.
- Don't stand too near the gates of a venue or event arena, as there could be a surge when they open.
- Hold onto railings when using stairways or escalators.
- Stand on dry, even ground so that you don't slip.
- Watch out for trash you could trip over.

- One of the primary signs that a crowd crush might occur is when officials seem overwhelmed and are struggling to control the crowd. Insufficient signage, barriers, and loudspeakers can also indicate trouble ahead.

Survival Decisions: GO

✓ Checklist for Safe and Effective Evacuation

❏ If you are attending an event that may attract a large crowd, note all potential exits, not only the one where you entered.

❏ As the crowd thickens, you might start to feel uneasy. If it's difficult to move your hands to touch your face, there are probably too many people in the space. If anything unexpected happens, you might get caught in a crush. Leave when you start feeling uncomfortable, although this might be a difficult decision, especially if your tickets were costly or you traveled some distance to the event.

❏ Move to the edges of the crowd while you still can. That way if something happens, you won't be caught in the densest part of the crowd.

❏ If you are caught in the crush, move with the crowd and stay on your feet until there is a lull when you can move toward the edges of the crush. You can hold the hand of someone who asks for help or of your companion if you are with someone else. Watch for an exit as you move.

Survival Decisions: STAY

✓ Checklist for Safe and Effective Staying

❏ Take cover.

❏ Look for a side hallway or closet.

❏ Seek out trees or vehicles—anything you can shelter behind or climb on to avoid the force of the crowd.

❏ When the crowd thins, escape through one of the alternative exits you identified when you entered the venue.

EARTHQUAKE

The earth's crust consists of tectonic plates floating above a deeper mantle. They move continuously but slowly. Their edges form natural fault lines. When neighboring plates slide past one another, this creates a strike-slip fault, such as California's San Andreas Fault.

Earthquakes are triggered when the rock bordering the fault becomes deformed due to the pressure exerted on it or from friction when plates don't slide smoothly past one another. The slab then breaks, triggering an abrupt movement and releasing seismic pressure waves that shake the ground. The place on the surface corresponding to the break is called the epicenter.

An earthquake's most visible impact results from ground vibrations. The seismic waves released by the earthquake make buildings quiver and move horizontally, potentially damaging them. If buildings are unable to withstand these forces, they can collapse.

When seismic waves pass through sandy soils near a water table, they can cause the groundwater to saturate the soil so that it behaves like a viscous liquid. This is called liquefaction. The water and sand may erupt like a geyser, causing flooding. Liquefaction destroys water and power lines and makes buildings tilt precariously even if they don't collapse. Earthquakes cause flooding when they compromise levees, dams, and reservoirs.

While strike-slip faults may cause landslides, most injuries are sustained when structures are damaged. Surface faulting can affect buildings, roads, and infrastructure such as water, gas, and sewer lines. When infrastructure breaks during an earthquake, flammable liquids released by broken lines may catch fire. Overturned stoves and broken fireplaces also cause earthquake fires. The combination of fires and broken water lines can be catastrophic.

In addition, tsunamis are underwater seismic waves triggered by earthquakes on the sea floor. Their wave height can sometimes rise to 100 feet. Because their wave crests can be very far apart, their energy doesn't dissipate in the surf. While earthquakes affect the area near the fault, tsunamis cause destruction miles from the quake's epicenter.

In the United States, you can view a US Geological Survey (USGS) National Seismic Hazard Map at USGS.gov/programs/earthquake-hazards/science/introduction-national-seismic-hazard-maps.

Immediate Action

Action depends on your location and circumstances. Follow these tips based on your location:

Indoors

- Remaining in a room inside a building reduces your chances of injury. Drop to the ground on your hands and knees.
- Turn off the stove and faucets.
- You are most likely to be injured by falling objects or breaking glass. Keep away from things that could break, move, or fall, especially windows, glass items, mirrors, hanging pictures, cabinets or closets with doors that could open, and fireplaces or chimneys (the earthquake could dislodge bricks). Quickly *drop, cover, and hold on.*
- Crawl under a sturdy table, desk, or similar furniture. Protecting your head and neck are crucial. Cover them with a pillow, cushion, or your arms.
- Hold onto the furniture and protect your head and neck until the shaking stops.
- If no sturdy furniture is available, lie next to an interior wall, covering your face and neck with your arms and hands.
- If you are in a wheelchair, stay in the room. Move away from windows, outer walls, hanging objects, and fireplaces. Lock the wheels and remove loose items from the chair. Protect your head and neck with a large pillow, heavy book, or your arms.
- If you are in a high-rise building, stay inside and move away from windows and outside walls. Never use the elevators, as the electricity might go off and you could be trapped. Sprinklers might go off.

In a Crowded Location

- Don't rush for the doors or gates—you could get caught in a stampede. Move away from items or structures that could fall on you. Avoid windows and glass. *Drop, cover, and hold on*, and find something to shield your face and neck from glass and falling objects.

In a Vehicle

- Find a place where there are no utility poles, tall trees, overhead wires, and under- or overpasses. Park on the shoulder, put on the parking brake, and remain in the vehicle.
- Turn on the radio for emergency broadcasts. If a utility pole or wire falls onto your vehicle, wait for a trained person to remove it before getting out.
- When it is safe to continue driving, proceed cautiously, as roads and bridges may be damaged, impassable, or blocked by debris.

Outside

- Don't run into a building. Falling debris and fixtures falling from buildings or doorways is a major risk, as are breaking windows, so avoid buildings. Move away from utility wires, sinkholes, trees, telephone poles, or fuel and gas lines. Once out in the open, drop to the ground and wait for the shaking to stop.
- If you are in a wheelchair, move away from trees, utility poles, and buildings. Lock your wheels and protect your head and neck as best you can. Wait for the shaking to stop.
- If you are near the shore, drop to the ground and wait for the shaking to stop. If the shaking continues for more than 20 seconds, a tsunami might have been triggered, so head for higher ground. If a tsunami is suspected, move inland as fast as you can and search for the highest location you can find other than the beach. Avoid fallen debris.

Survival Decisions: GO

It's not advisable to move from your location during an earthquake. These natural disasters happen suddenly, and there won't be time to evacuate.

Survival Decisions: STAY

Ensure that your entire household knows how to *drop, cover, and hold on* during earthquakes. Have regular drills so that everyone knows where to shelter and what to do. Near the coast, have a tsunami evacuation plan. Know where high ground, a safe area, or the nearest tsunami vertical evacuation refuge is located, together with the quickest route.

✓ Checklist for Safe and Effective Staying

❑ Immediately follow the previously listed steps based on your location.

❑ Monitor emergency information from authorities on your NOAA Weather Radio or NOAA-compatible two-way radios. Do not leave before the all clear.

ECONOMIC COLLAPSE OR RECESSION

An economic collapse is when the regional or national economy breaks down for an extended period. Reduced trade volumes, currency volatility, unrest, social breakdown, and reduced law and order are characteristic. The collapse often follows an economic downturn, recession, or depression. Currencies may devalue or even be replaced. Political unrest and coups often result from an economic collapse.

Signs of economic collapse include:

- Soaring interest rates
- Currency devaluations due to reduced investor confidence
- A global currency crisis, which is when a major international currency such as the US dollar loses value

Many small businesses are more exposed to bankruptcy during an economic collapse and/or recession. Larger businesses also suffer during recessions. Companies freeze hiring and restrict salary increases and bonuses. Marketing and advertising budgets may contract. During an economic collapse, companies shed numerous jobs. They may also have difficulty servicing debt and obtaining loans.

Immediate Action

Economic downturns, recessions, and even a complete economic collapse are slow-onset disasters. If you are watching trends, you should not be taken by surprise. However, if a collapse occurs suddenly due to a political meltdown or unexpected event, such as corruption within the markets, there are things you can do to soften the blow:

- Begin to think about things other than currency that you may be able to barter. These include food production, trade skills (plumbing, electricity, construction, etc.), clean water, firewood, medical services, and other products and goods.
- Reduce costs by negotiating better terms with anyone you purchase items from.
- Ask your creditors for more flexible terms.
- Cut all unnecessary spending.
- Consider developing multiple streams of income either through starting a small business, selling goods, or performing services.
- Create a spending budget and stick to it.

Survival Decisions: GO

The next recession is likely to be global, and many countries are already feeling the effects of economic downturns. When things get tough and options diminish, it's tempting to consider relocating. You could move either to another town or city in your state or to another state. Alternatively, you could take the plunge and move to another country altogether. You'll need to consider this very carefully, as things may not necessarily be better elsewhere, and you might have to leave your support networks behind.

Factors supporting evacuation during an economic collapse:

- You have better opportunities and more security in a new town, state, or country.
- You've conducted all the proper research to make a wise and educated decision.
- You've lined up work and completed all paperwork and are approved to relocate.

✓ Checklist for Safe and Effective Evacuation

❏ Obtain as much information as you can about the region or country you intend to go to, including their immigration, employment, business, and tax policies, as well as options concerning housing, schooling, and health benefits.

❏ Have work lined up before you leave.

❏ Upskill if you don't have the required qualifications. Some countries might need you to have a local qualification, so ensure that you have the right types of qualifications. Sometimes experience won't be enough.

❏ Sort out your finances so that you can afford to immigrate. Ensure that you can settle outstanding taxes and pay for visas and residence and work permits, movers, and other costs related to immigration.

Relocating doesn't always equal success or happiness, so do your due diligence and ensure that you will be happy with your decision.

Survival Decisions: STAY

Factors supporting staying during an economic collapse:

• You don't have better opportunities and more security in a new town, state, or country.
• You haven't conducted all the proper research to make a wise and educated decision.
• You haven't lined up work and completed all paperwork and are not approved to relocate.

✓ Checklist for Safe and Effective Staying

❑ Diversify your income by monetizing existing hobbies and skills, picking up part-time employment, or starting a small business.

❑ Network with others as much as possible. Make them aware of your struggles and let them know you are looking for ideas to help improve your situation. Become active in faith-based organizations or civic groups to help build a support community, potentially share resources, and also foster feelings of connection and belonging.

❑ Take time to develop valuable trade skills or invest time in developing a renewable source of bartering such as backyard chickens, dairy goats, or a vegetable garden.

❑ Tighten up spending as much as possible. Only purchase what is necessary and negotiate for better prices when possible.

❑ Refine your budget each week and spend wisely.

❑ Do not take on additional debt.

ELECTRICAL GRID FAILURE

The United States could soon be facing an electricity shortage due to increased demand from technology like cryptocurrencies, electric vehicles, and artificial intelligence. America's electricity infrastructure is aging, potentially exacerbating the problem. Infrastructure has been compromised at times by climate change impacts, and as the weather becomes hotter, pressure in the grid is likely to mount, increasing the likelihood of outages.

The US and Canada share a highly interconnected electricity grid. Other units can pick up the slack if one goes down. During excessively high demand, this may not be possible and blackouts may result. If too many areas in the grid are compromised, then sections of it can trip, causing blackouts. High winds, lightning strikes, and heavy snowfall are most often implicated in outages in the US. The grid is also vulnerable to an electromagnetic pulse (EMP), cyberattacks, or physical attacks on power stations, substations, and transformers, causing overloads and blackouts.

An industrialized nation relies on electricity to function effectively. Complete grid failure would:

- Prevent oil and gas refining and distribution.
- Compromise water purification and supply, together with the removal and treatment of wastewater.
- Stop pumps required for irrigation, impacting food production.
- Prevent pumps and pipelines from delivering gasoline and other fuels, affecting farming, delivery of food and goods, and transportation.
- Disrupt road networks due to traffic signals not working.
- Disrupt production at plants that manufacture fertilizers, pesticides, and animal feed; manufacturing outlets; and mines.
- Shut off refrigerators and freezers, compromising food storage.
- Disrupt banking and financial services, including ATMs.
- Disrupt communications networks.

Immediate Action

If you experience a power outage, do the following:

- Turn off all electrical appliances so that they won't be damaged if there is a surge when the power returns.
- Check whether the outage is isolated to just your house or if it is neighborhood-wide.
- Contact your utility to notify them and find out how long the outage will last.
- Avoid downed power lines if you go out, and report them to your utility.
- Keep refrigerator and freezer doors closed so that food does not spoil.
- Get out your rechargeable camping lights, headlamps, and flashlights.
- If you have backup power, such as a generator, set it up and ensure that it is working properly.
- Never use charcoal grills, propane grills, or generators indoors, as you may be overcome by carbon monoxide fumes. Ensure that generator exhaust faces away from the house and do not operate generators close to windows or doors.
- If the weather is cold, implement a backup heat plan and insulate exposed pipes to prevent freezing. Turn faucets on to drip.
- Avoid traveling, as a grid outage causes confusion and chaos.
- Expect disruptions in normal facilities such as grocery stores, hospitals, banks, and more.
- Cell phone networks may be affected, so you may not be able to make calls. If not, execute the Family Communications Plan.
- Prepare for using stored food, water, and backup cooking methods.

Survival Decisions: GO

It's highly unlikely that you would need to evacuate your home during a power outage, unless it's combined with a flood or winter storm, in which case follow the recommendations given in those entries.

Survival Decisions: STAY

Factors supporting staying during power outage include:

- There are no weather-related issues that require evacuation.
- There are no other issues that require evacuation besides not having power.

✓ Checklist for Safe and Effective Staying

- ❏ Take stock of all advance preparations such as food, water, prescription medicines, and more to create a timeline for how long you can independently survive if the grid does not come back up soon.
- ❏ Conserve fuel if using it for backup heat or cooking.
- ❏ Conserve all resources, including power, food, and water.
- ❏ Stay informed using a NOAA Weather Radio, which will also broadcast emergency information about the grid failure.
- ❏ Implement an off-grid communications plan with family and friends using your ham or GMRS two-way radios.
- ❏ Review Chapter 10 on protection and self-defense, as crime will increase during a grid-down event.
- ❏ Install solar-powered security lights if you haven't already.
- ❏ Consider sleeping in shifts with other family members if crime increases or is suspected.
- ❏ Implement any backup food production plans such as sprouting, growing a vegetable garden, or raising livestock.
- ❏ Continue to develop products and services that can be used to barter with others. Trade skills, medical supplies, and food production are at the top of the list.

EXPLOSION

Although explosions are of short duration, the pressure waves they create are much higher than those emanating from natural causes such as earthquakes or high winds. Explosive pressures reduce as they radiate out from the source. In urban areas, however, reflections off surrounding buildings may spread the damage more widely.

The air-blast shock wave generated by an explosion causes most of the damage. Structures, including exterior walls, windows, floors, columns, and even girders may crack, buckle, or break. An entire building may be engulfed by a pressure wave after an explosion so that the structure rapidly collapses. Explosions shatter glass, and damage may occur some distance from the source after a significant outdoor explosion. Injuries from flying glass and from glass falling from buildings onto streets are common. Those closest to the explosion may experience ruptured eardrums, collapsed lungs, blunt trauma injuries, and cuts or lacerations from glass and masonry fragments.

Immediate Action

Explosions happen suddenly, and there is little time to prepare. They are often associated with fires, floods, or power outages. Take the following action:

- If you are inside a building when an explosion detonates, take cover under a desk, table, or other heavy furniture to shield yourself from flying glass and other debris.
- Remain inside until you've determined it is safe to leave. Never use elevators.
- Grab your bug out bag and any of the 8 Ps of evacuation you can gather quickly.
- Dial 911.
- Find a safe emergency gathering place or begin to implement your evacuation plan.

- Report any further hazards or details about those who were in the building with you.
- Stay calm and follow the instructions of emergency officials.

Survival Decisions: GO

Factors supporting evacuation during an explosion include:

- Your home is directly affected by the explosion or otherwise susceptible to damage.
- Authorities have issued an evacuation order.
- You know of or see suspicious activity.
- Post-explosion hazards such as chemical exposure or water pollutants exist.

✓ Checklist for Safe and Effective Evacuation

- ❏ If you are not directly affected by the explosion, don't rush toward the scene, as you could impede emergency responders or be caught in a second explosion. Leave the area without delay.
- ❏ Evacuate as soon as debris stops falling and things are quiet.
- ❏ Grab your bug out bag and leave. Do not take time to gather other personal items.
- ❏ Watch for weakened floors and stairways.
- ❏ Never use elevators.
- ❏ Look for signs of smoke. If there is smoke, get beneath it by crawling. This is where the most oxygen is.
- ❏ When you are outside, let first responders know if there are any other people or pets inside.
- ❏ Get far away from the scene.

Survival Decisions: STAY

Factors supporting staying during an explosion include:

- You are unable to escape.
- There are mobility issues with someone in your party.
- It is too dangerous to leave the premises due to the aftermath of the explosion.
- You are trapped under debris.
- The exit has been cut off.

✓ Checklist for Safe and Effective Staying

- ❏ Call 911 and explain what has happened. Stay on the line until help arrives.
- ❏ Remain beneath your table or desk for protection, as more explosions may detonate.
- ❏ Avoid windows, glass, mirrors, overhead fittings, bookcases, filing cabinets, and electrical equipment.
- ❏ Don't use matches or lighters in case there is a gas leak.
- ❏ If there are smoke and fire outside, close internal doors between you and the fire; wedge a cotton cloth along the bottom of the door to keep out the smoke; and stay low, as there is more oxygen close to the floor.
- ❏ If you are caught beneath fallen debris, use a flashlight, whistle, or tap on a pipe to let emergency officials know that you are there.
- ❏ Cover your nose and mouth with a cotton cloth to avoid inhaling excessive dust.
- ❏ Shout only as a last resort, as this uses energy and will draw more dust into your lungs.

EXTREME HEAT

Heat waves are persistent, unusually high temperatures caused by an atmospheric high-pressure system forcing warm air to the ground. Heat waves are becoming more common due to climate change and kill more people in the US than any other weather-related event.

Extremely hot weather can cause dehydration, heat exhaustion, and heat stroke. Heat strokes can be fatal and exacerbate preexisting health issues such as diabetes or heart conditions. Excessive heat can also cause kidney problems, skin infections, and premature births.

Immediate Action

The main difficulties with extreme heat are keeping hydrated and staying cool. Use any resource available to hydrate and cool down including:

- Relocating to a shaded or air-conditioned space.
- Applying cool, wet towels to skin to reduce temperature.
- Submerging your body in cool but not cold water.
- Setting up fans in your space.
- Opening windows to increase airflow.

Survival Decisions: STAY

Factors supporting staying in place during extreme heat include:

- Your home is well equipped to deal with extreme heat, such as having fans and air-conditioning.

✓ Checklist for Safe and Effective Staying

❏ Listen to weather forecasts and government warnings.

❏ Do essential activities early in the day, when it's cooler.

❏ Wear a hat and sunscreen and stay in the shade if you go outside.

❏ Use air-conditioning or visit air-conditioned buildings like shopping centers or libraries.

❏ Close curtains and blinds to prevent the sun from shining into rooms.

❏ Electric fans can cool the body when inside temperatures are below 104°F.

❏ Soak a towel in cold tap water and wrap it loosely around your head.

❏ Spray cool water on your skin.

❏ Wrap ice cubes in a damp towel and coil it loosely around your neck.

❏ Take cool showers and foot baths.

❏ Wear light, loose-fitting clothing.

❏ Drink water before you feel thirsty, especially if you are doing physical activity outdoors. Avoid sweet, caffeinated, or alcoholic drinks. Sports drinks containing electrolytes help replenish salts lost to perspiration.

❏ Take a water bottle when you leave home.

❏ Watch for signs of dehydration, including thirst; lightheadedness; dry mouth; feeling tired; having dark, concentrated urine; or passing less urine than usual.

❏ Check on family members and friends.

❏ Do not leave pets or children in closed vehicles or rooms.

❏ Ensure that children wear loose, lightweight clothing and are drinking enough water.

❏ Don't allow children to play outside in the heat of the day.

Survival Decisions: GO

During heat waves, you won't evacuate but may need to visit a friend's or relative's house and even a public cooling center. Cooling centers are air-conditioned public spaces where people can obtain relief from the heat. Cooling centers are open locally in some areas when:

- The National Weather Service issues an excessive heat warning, or a Heat-Risk level 3 warning for over three days.
- Overnight low temperatures are forecast to be 75°F or more.
- An electrical or energy emergency is declared.

The centers are established by local authorities in public spaces including churches, town halls, libraries, and similar facilities. Those at risk for heat-related illnesses or experiencing heat stress receive priority.

FLOODING

Flooding occurs when normally dry areas become inundated with water due to heavy rain, snowmelt, or unusually high tides. Floods may last a few hours or days. The most dangerous are flash floods, caused by heavy rainfall over a short period, snowmelt, an ice jam, or a dam wall failure. These are particularly hazardous in urban areas, where concrete and paved areas increase runoff.

Flooding causes drowning fatalities and damages property, infrastructure, and crops. It disrupts business, transport, and education. Floods may contaminate water supplies and sever people from amenities and community services. They drown wildlife, erode riverbanks and beaches, and spread diseases and environmental contaminants.

Immediate Action

A flood watch indicates that flooding or flash flooding is possible. Pay attention to the weather and prepare to move to higher ground. If a flood or flash flood warning is issued, flooding is imminent or occurring. Take immediate action by following these steps.

Survival Decisions: STAY

Factors supporting staying in place during a flood include:

- You cannot evacuate for any reason.
- Authorities recommend staying in place (only if their reasoning makes sense).

✓ Checklist for Safe and Effective Staying

❑ Use NOAA Weather Radio to monitor flood activity. Listen to news reports for emergency updates and instructions.

❑ Cancel outdoor activities, deliveries, and courier collections.

- ❑ Contact your insurance broker to discuss claims procedures.
- ❑ Go inside with your pets.
- ❑ Keep your bug out bag and important documents, cash, and valuables with you.

If the water rises to dangerous levels:

- ❑ Go to the highest level of the building or onto the roof.
- ❑ Avoid attics, as you can be trapped by rising waters.
- ❑ Fill up your vehicle's gas tank.
- ❑ Establish emergency communications for your family.
- ❑ Unplug sensitive electronic equipment and appliances—do not do this if they are wet or you are standing in water.
- ❑ Check that your sump pump is working.
- ❑ Elevate or move furniture and belongings to an upper floor.
- ❑ Elevate hazardous substances.
- ❑ Fill containers with drinking water.
- ❑ Place sandbags around doors and windows and where water might collect.
- ❑ Plug sinks, baths, and toilets to prevent water from bubbling up.
- ❑ If you are in a high-rise building, avoid elevators, as the power may go off and you could be trapped.
- ❑ Prepare blankets, warm clothing, and rain gear.
- ❑ Prepare for evacuation.

Survival Decisions: GO

Factors supporting evacuation during a flood include:

- You or your loved ones are in imminent danger.
- You question the structural integrity of your home or location.
- Authorities recommend evacuation.
- You are not prepared to be cut off from utilities, food, water, and medical help for an undetermined amount of time.

✓ Checklist for Safe and Effective Evacuation

- ❏ Implement your Family Communications Plan.
- ❏ Implement your evacuation plan; choose a route and destination based on flood activity.
- ❏ Never walk or drive on flooded roads or cross flooded waterways or bridges—turn around, don't drown.
- ❏ Stay in the vehicle if it washes into floodwaters; if it starts filling with water, get onto the roof.
- ❏ Top off your vehicle's fuel tank with stored fuel.
- ❏ Prepare your evacuation vehicle by packing the 8 Ps of evacuation.
- ❏ If you do not own a vehicle, connect with your previously chosen mode of transport.
- ❏ Unplug all electronics. Refrigerators and freezers can also be unplugged if flooding is a risk.
- ❏ Secure all doors and windows.
- ❏ Turn off utilities, including water, gas, and electricity.
- ❏ Consider installing the inflatable Toilet Stopper from Floodshield.com in all toilets to prevent sewage backflow through the toilets.
- ❏ Wear sturdy, protective shoes and clothing and a hat. Pack rain gear.

FOREIGN INVASION OR WAR

A war is a violent conflict between nations or countries. Warfare is detrimental and costly, so nations usually resort to this form of conflict resolution only if other avenues have been exhausted. Prolonged conflicts are usually avoided due to the high costs.

Today's wars are complex, taking place on land, on sea, and in air, and now also in cyberspace. Hackers may impede communications and command and control systems and shut down civilian institutions and infrastructure, increasing a nation's vulnerability. Drones are increasingly being used for surveillance and to carry and deploy weapons. Artificial intelligence analyzes enemy deployments and develops counterstrategies.

Immediate Action

Armed conflicts can escalate quickly, undermining your safety. Following are some strategies to keep you and your family safe as the situation deteriorates:

- Be careful about disinformation and get information from reputable sources and people you trust.
- Talk to your family about leaving or staying. Keep your plans fluid in case the situation changes. Bear in mind that it may become difficult to get flights out if the conflict escalates, in which case you might need to leave by vehicle or on foot—and there might be a lot of people leaving by then.
- Stay indoors in a safe place and don't go out more than you need to.
- When you do go out:
    - Ensure that your area and the route you plan to take are safe.
    - Organize transport in advance if necessary.
    - Find out which roads are closed.
    - Keep a low profile.
    - Be alert and aware, especially in large crowds.
    - Have emergency contact numbers on your phone.
    - If you notice anything suspicious, leave immediately.

- Avoid demonstrations, large crowds, or large numbers of armed forces.
- Don't take pictures of armed forces or local authorities.

- Be careful what you store on your phone, as you could be linked to unpopular social views or political causes.
- Store your important papers, some cash, and valuables in a sealable box and put it in a safe place.
- Move into a sturdy brick building with a basement capable of withstanding bombardments. Find one you can seal up in the event of chemical leaks or attacks. Alternatively, build an insulated shelter if you live in a wooded area.
- Don't get into fights and arguments.
- Defend yourself when necessary and have a weapon available if possible.
- Move away if the conflict gets too close to your home. Travel to a safe zone designated by the authorities or to rural areas. However, it may be more difficult to receive aid in a rural area, and you may need basic survival skills.
- Keep yourself clean to avoid infections.
- Treat cuts and abrasions quickly.
- Stay positive and maintain your connections to friends and family.

Survival Decisions: GO

Factors supporting evacuation during foreign invasion include:

- Humanitarian aid runs out or nongovernmental organizations (NGOs) are unable to reach the area due to bombardments.
- Everyday items become hard to get.
- Your home becomes damaged or ruined.
- Hospitals become overcrowded, understaffed, or contaminated.
- The water supply becomes compromised.
- You lose your job or means of providing for your family.
- It is too dangerous to stay because of conflict.

✔ Checklist for Safe and Effective Evacuation

❏ Implement your Family Communications Plan.

❏ You may not need to leave the country. Start off by moving to an area beyond the conflict zone.

❏ Implement your evacuation plan; choose a route and destination based on known conflict activity.

❏ Top off your vehicle's fuel tank with stored fuel.

❏ Prepare your evacuation vehicle by packing the 8 Ps of evacuation.

❏ Secure all doors and windows.

❏ Turn on your headlights.

❏ Monitor NOAA Weather Radio and news broadcasts for emergency updates.

❏ If possible, travel in a caravan with friends or other evacuees. There is strength in numbers, especially if there is a simultaneous breakdown in law and order.

❏ Dress and behave in what is called gray man. This means to look as average as possible by wearing muted colors. Avoid anything that looks militaristic or tactical.

❏ Women and girls should do everything possible to not call attention to their being female. This includes loose-fitting clothing, hats, and bulky jackets.

❏ Instead of tactical bug out bags, consider packing your emergency supplies in low-key school backpacks or tote bags.

❏ Stay on the road with other vehicles that are also evacuating.

❏ If stopped by enemy forces, comply with requests for identification. Do not draw attention.

❏ Travel during the day if at all possible.

❏ Do not interact with anyone, especially strangers, unless absolutely necessary.

Survival Decisions: STAY

Factors supporting staying during foreign invasion include:

- It becomes too late.
- Humanitarian aid is sufficient.
- You are able to meet your needs and obtain everyday items.
- Your home is not damaged or ruined.

✓ Checklist for Safe and Effective Staying

❏ Plan for evacuation by identifying routes and locations just in case an opportunity presents itself.

❏ Prepare and pack the 8 Ps of evacuation.

❏ Plan for disruptions in power, food, and medical and water supplies. Use your stores accordingly and implement any long-term food production strategies you have planned for.

❏ Learn how to protect yourself and obtain weapons for doing so. The presence of enemy forces will likely mean that there is no existing law and order.

❏ Identify escape routes out of the immediate area and the country in case you need to leave.

❏ Withdraw cash from the bank as soon as possible.

❏ Set up a rain barrel to harvest rainwater from your roof.

❏ Ration available food.

❏ Begin to consider hunting and wild foraging as options for food procurement.

❏ Ration all toiletries, medicines, and hygiene products.

❏ Stock up on basic medicines and first aid supplies.

❏ Maintain proper hygiene to prevent infections.

❏ Eat as healthily as you can to improve your resilience.

❏ Build an alliance of friends, neighbors, and others who can help each other out in times of need.

❏ Implement off-grid communications such as two-way radios.

HOME INVASION

A home invasion is when a perpetrator enters someone's home or apartment when they are there, often at night. This is different from a burglary, which happens when the occupants are out.

Home invasions are often violent. The person forces his way in, drawing attention to himself, and must then subdue the occupants. Perpetrators are often armed with firearms or knives and carry ropes or duct tape to restrain their victims. They sometimes pose as law enforcement or utility company employees and force their way in when the homeowner opens the door. Home invasions often create negative psychological effects because we consider our homes to be sanctuaries and can have profound post-traumatic stress implications.

Immediate Actions

Home invasions can happen anytime. Perpetrators have often been observing the occupants for some time to establish their schedules and vulnerability. Obtaining money, drugs, or valuables is the normal objective. Perpetrators choose to enter homes while they are occupied so that the owners can find these items for them. If your home is invaded, do the following:

- Keep quiet and stay where you are. Moving about will draw the criminals' attention.
- Lock the door of the room you are in.
- Listen to establish why the person is in your home.
- Text other residents to notify them of the invasion. However, if people are sleeping, leave them be, as they might awaken and alarm the intruders.
- Keep pets under control.
- Call 911 or your local police.
- Avoid confronting the intruders, as this could escalate the situation.
- If the intruders run off, don't pursue them but note their direction so that you can tell the police.
- Don't try and save your possessions.

- Do not retaliate unless you are trained to do so.
- Be quiet to avoid making the intruders more tense or encouraging them to turn on you.
- Take notes that will assist law enforcement.

Survival Decisions: GO

Factors supporting fleeing during a home invasion include:

- You have an escape option that will not draw the intruders' attention.
- You have verified that there is no accomplice outside.
- You are not leaving behind loved ones.

Survival Decisions: STAY

✓ Checklist for Safe and Effective Staying

- ❏ Listen to establish the intruders' location in the house and their activities.
- ❏ Try to get your family to a safe area. Lock the door and barricade it if possible to buy you time.
- ❏ Call 911.
- ❏ Remain in place until law enforcement arrives.
- ❏ Use weapons if necessary. Prepare to use a firearm if you have one.

HURRICANE

Hurricanes begin as low-pressure tropical weather systems characterized by showers and thunderstorms. Winds start circulating around the center, creating a cloud cluster or tropical disturbance. As the storm grows, the upper air cools and destabilizes, while the winds inside the column strengthen. When wind speeds reach 74 mph, the storm becomes a hurricane. Wind speeds determine its intensity. A Category 2 hurricane has strong winds with speeds up to 110 mph, while a Category 4 hurricane has extremely dangerous winds with speeds up to 156 mph.

When a hurricane makes landfall, several events may intensify its effects, including:

- Heavy downpours, damaging winds, and tornadoes.
- Flooding in coastal towns and low-lying areas, causing beach erosion, uprooted trees, floating boulders, and flood debris.
- A destructive surge of ocean water—the storm surge, which may temporarily raise sea levels by 30 feet or more, submerging buildings and infrastructure, especially at high tide.
- Flooding as the hurricane moves inland.

Immediate Action

Hurricane watches are issued 48 hours before storms make landfall, while warnings are given 36 hours beforehand. If you receive these warnings, do the following:

- Monitor the news and social media to stay informed of developments.
- Follow instructions given by the authorities, especially if you are in an evacuation zone.
- Consult FEMA flood maps to establish whether your home falls within a flood-prone area. If so, prepare to evacuate.

- Locate your Family Communications Plan and connect with all family members.
- Begin to prepare for evacuation.
- Locate and prepare all bug out bags.
- Assemble all 8 Ps of evacuation.
- Put important documents, cash, and valuables in a waterproof pouch and store it safely.
- Designate a windowless indoor space where you can ride out the storm if necessary.
- Use stored fuel to fill up your vehicle's gas tank.

You should prepare for power outages by:

- Locating flashlights and spare batteries.
- Charging cell phones and electronics while power is still available.
- Setting the refrigerator and freezer to their coldest settings.
- Filling your bathtub with water to use for flushing toilets.
- Preparing your generator or other backup power system.

You can prepare your home by:

- Bringing in outdoor furniture, trash cans, children's toys, and other items that may blow or wash away.
- Ensuring that rain gutters and downpipes are clear.
- Covering all windows with storm shutters, ⅝-inch exterior-grade plywood or marine plywood, or Hurricane Fabric.
- Turning off propane tanks not in use.
- Preparing tools for turning off your gas or electricity at the main valve or switch in case you decide to evacuate.
- Parking vehicles in your garage (if available) and ensuring that all have the proper emergency kit items.

Survival Decisions: GO

You might need to evacuate if ordered to by the authorities or if your home won't withstand a hurricane. You might choose to leave if you are at risk from storm surges or in a low-lying, flood-prone area. Evacuate immediately if ordered, as you might not have much time. Use routes recommended by officials. Bear in mind that you may need to evacuate on foot.

Evacuation can and does prevent casualties. Drownings are a major cause of death during and after hurricanes. Factors supporting evacuation during a hurricane include:

- Your home or location is not suitable to withstand a storm surge or high winds.
- Authorities have issued a recommended or mandatory evacuation order.
- You are in an area susceptible to flooding.
- You have established safer location options.
- Routes are clear—getting out early could be wise.
- You are not prepared to be cut off from utilities, food, water, and medical help for an undetermined amount of time.

✓ Checklist for Safe and Effective Evacuation

- ❑ Implement your Family Communications Plan.
- ❑ Implement your evacuation plan.
- ❑ Top off your vehicle's fuel tank with stored fuel.
- ❑ Prepare your evacuation vehicle by packing the 8 Ps of evacuation.
- ❑ If you do not own a vehicle, connect with your previously chosen mode of transport.
- ❑ Unplug all electronics. Refrigerators and freezers can also be unplugged if flooding is a risk.
- ❑ Secure all doors and windows.
- ❑ Turn off utilities.
- ❑ Wear sturdy, protective shoes and clothing and a hat. Pack rain gear.

Survival Decisions: STAY

If you are unable to evacuate, you may need to shelter in place. Keep your bug out bag with you. If your area is threatened by flooding or storm surges, go to the highest level of the building. Avoid attics, as you may become trapped by floodwaters. Mobile homes are not robust enough for sheltering from hurricanes, so you will need to find sturdier accommodations before the storm arrives. Relocate to a sturdy structure on higher ground, as you may be unable to move once the storm arrives.

If your home is not threatened by flooding or a storm surge, go to a small, windowless room on a level least likely to be flooded. Do not leave the premises until officials give the all clear.

Factors supporting staying in place during a hurricane include:

- Your location is suitable to withstanding a hurricane (construction preparations have been made in advance).
- You don't have enough time to evacuate.
- Evacuation routes are blocked or limited.
- There are vulnerable people within your home for whom evacuation may present an immediate health risk.

✓ Checklist for Safe and Effective Staying

❑ Board up (or use Hurricane Fabric on) your windows and glass doors, as this will protect you from glass and flying debris.

❑ Retrieve your bug out bags and emergency survival kits.

❑ Fill any extra containers, including the bathtub, with water, in addition to your already stored water.

❑ Go inside as soon as possible and take your pets with you.

❑ Wind velocity increases with height—if you need to shelter in a high-rise, shelter at the lowest level that won't be affected by flooding.

❑ Inland areas can also be affected by flooding due to high precipitation.

❑ Save calls for emergencies.

❑ Use generators outdoors and well away from windows.

❑ Monitor current emergency information and instructions.

KIDNAPPING OR ABDUCTION

Kidnapping is the seizing and holding of an individual against their will. The purpose is usually to demand a ransom or to manipulate or control the kidnapped person. The victim is forced, threatened, or deceived into going with the perpetrator. Kidnapping is a criminal offense and often involves minor children.

Abduction involves not only kidnapping but also the intention to commit other offenses. Abduction is linked to human trafficking, forced marriage, or a noncustodial parent taking a minor child for visitation and then not returning them. False imprisonment is also considered a form of abduction.

Immediate Action

If someone tries to kidnap or abduct you:

- Make as big of a scene as you can.
- Do everything in your power to resist. Kidnappers often choose soft targets, so if you resist and fight hard, you have a good chance of not being taken captive. Kick, bite, and scratch. Pull away and run for the nearest building or group of people.
- Look for nearby items that can be used as weapons: furniture, rocks, bricks, chunks of masonry, bottle caps, glass shards, or even sand that can be thrown into the perpetrator's face. Use everything you can to aid you in your fight. Remember, your life could be at stake.
- If there are people nearby, shout to draw attention to yourself. You can shout for help or yell "Fire." This might also distract the kidnappers, giving you a chance to escape. Shout for someone to call the police.
- Never get into a vehicle, as you might be driven a long distance, making you harder to find. Even if you are captured, fight to free yourself and escape.

Kidnap Prevention Tips

There's very little you can do to prepare for a kidnapping or abduction, but you can minimize your risks. Follow these guidelines:

- When you go out, always tell someone where you're going and when you will be back.
- Take off your earbuds and put your phone away so that you can hear and see everything around you.
- Travel or walk in groups and keep at least 3 feet between all people and the road margin to provide a safe distance from vehicles.
- Stay on well-lit pedestrian sidewalks and don't take shortcuts. Walk near banks, places with CCTV and security guards, and late-night convenience stores.
- If a vehicle or motorcycle slows near you, move off fast. Put as much distance as possible between the vehicle and you.
- If you see anything unusual, call 911.
- Kidnappers watch their victims to establish their schedules. Vary your routine. Take different routes and don't leave your home or workplace at the same time every day.
- Never get into a stranger's vehicle, no matter how plausible their story or if they offer you a lift. If someone stops to ask you a question, answer and move off. If you feel uncomfortable, leave immediately.
- Avoid unsafe areas.
- Know exactly where you are going and how to get there.
- Know where the police and fire stations are located. If you are overseas, know the address of your nearest embassy or consulate and how to reach it from your accommodation.
- Invest in pepper spray and keep it in easy reach when you are out.
- If someone tries to grab you, plant your feet firmly on the ground, legs spread and knees slightly bent.
- Put your key or keys between your fingers as you walk. If someone tries to grab you, punch them in the face with that hand. This should give you time to run off.

- If an attacker is holding you, focus on the parts of your body that are free and aim them at their knees, solar plexus, groin, throat, nose, or eyes. Use your feet if your arms are being held or your hands if they have you by the waist.

Survival Decisions: GO

✓ Checklist for Safe and Effective Evacuation from an Attempted Kidnapping

❑ Put as much distance between you and your captors as you can. If they are not chasing you, try not to run, as this will draw attention. Walk quickly and blend in with other pedestrians. If they are chasing you, make a commotion to attract the attention of others who may help you.

❑ Arm yourself. Pick up a stick or put a stone into a sock so that you have a weapon if your captors find you and try to recapture you.

❑ Find a drugstore or equivalent and treat any injuries you might have sustained.

❑ Attend to your physical needs. You may be thirsty or hungry or have insufficiently warm clothing, depending on your location, the time of day, and how long you were held.

❑ Find a phone somewhere and communicate. Dial 911 or any other emergency service.

❑ Find transportation so that you can go back to your home or hotel.

Survival Decisions: STAY

✓ Checklist for Safe and Effective Staying

❑ Stop fighting once you are overpowered, or you could be put into restraints or knocked out. Follow your captor's instructions and remain compliant. Evaluate your surroundings so that you can escape at a later stage.

- ❏ If you are taken somewhere in a vehicle and are able to see where you are going, note landmarks, road signs, and highway numbers so that you can find your way back if you escape. Try and estimate the time the trip takes.

- ❏ If you are in the trunk of a vehicle, look for the inside release handle so that you can climb out. If the vehicle doesn't have a release handle or you can't find it, kick out a taillight and wave your hands to alert other motorists that you are inside.

- ❏ Maintain your composure. Stay calm and don't cry or beg to be freed. Speak softly but clearly. Don't antagonize your captors, or you may be injured, restrained, or killed.

- ❏ Calmly ask for anything you need. Avoid talking about politics or religion, as an extremist group may be involved in your kidnapping.

- ❏ Observe the environment where you are being held. Note how many people are holding you, what they look like, and any exits from the room or building. If you are blindfolded, listen for sounds to indicate where you are, such as highway traffic, or distinctive smells. Feel around you to determine whether anything has sharp edges or there is something you could use to free yourself if you are restrained.

- ❏ Work out who seems to be in charge and make a mental note of the name or names they are using.

- ❏ Wait to be rescued unless you are certain that you can escape safely and without discovery. If you are caught trying to escape, your captors will deal severely with you and may kill you. If they are threatening to kill you, then you need to escape as soon as you can.

- ❏ If you are rescued, follow the authorities' directions. Get onto the ground and don't make any sudden movements, as they may not know who the captives and kidnappers are in the early stages. Don't run. Let them handcuff you, but make it clear that you are the victim.

LANDSLIDE

Landslides occur when rocks, boulders, mud, dirt, and vegetation slide or tumble down a slope. Mudslides are mobilized by water and often move through a streambed or canyon. These events may happen quickly or slowly. Volcanoes, earthquakes, and heavy rains following dry periods can trigger landslides.

Landslides can injure or kill people, bury homes, damage infrastructure, block roads, silt up harbors, break utility lines, and disrupt communications. Water can collect behind a debris field to create a dam, which can break, causing flooding. Transport can be disrupted due to road closures. Homes are rarely insured against landslides.

Immediate Action

Landslides often happen if there has been heavy rain, snow is melting fast, or your property is in an at-risk area. There is often a history of landslides in areas where landslides are likely.

During conditions and time frames when there is an immediate threat of landslide, do the following:

- Stay alert and don't go to sleep. Sleep in shifts as a family. Deaths while sleeping are common during landslides.
- Monitor weather reports and local news during heavy rainfall events so that you can establish whether landslides are occurring in your area.
- Contact your local fire, police, or public works department to assess potential dangers.
- Prepare for evacuation.

Signs to look for that a landslide may likely happen include:

- Drastic changes (either more or less) in water flow and clarity in nearby streams or waterways.

- The walls, patios, or porches of your home changing or moving in some way or odd structural behavior from other structures on your property such as shaking, trembling, or undulating.
- Leaning fences, poles, and trees.
- Sounds of rocks knocking together or trees cracking (could indicate that the soil is moving).

Survival Decisions: STAY

Factors supporting staying in place during a landslide include:

- Authorities have not issued an evacuation order.
- Your home is not in the path or near the path of a potential landslide.
- You've made advance preparations to shelter in place without access to food, water, power, and medical facilities for an undetermined period of time.
- Evacuation routes are blocked.
- Your home is of solid construction and made to withstand the force of a landslide.

✔ Checklist for Safe and Effective Staying

- ❏ Move to the second story of the building or higher if you can.
- ❏ Take shelter in a small interior room with no outside walls. Close the door.

Survival Decisions: GO

Factors supporting evacuation during a landslide include:

- Authorities have issued an evacuation order.
- Your home is located in or near the path of a potential landslide.
- You have not made advance preparations with food, water, or backup power to live for a few days off the grid.

- Your home or building construction is not conducive to withstanding the force of a landslide.
- There is a history of landslides in your location.
- Your home is located in or near an area particularly susceptible to landslides.

✓ Checklist for Safe and Effective Evacuation

- ❑ Implement your Family Communications Plan.
- ❑ Implement your evacuation plan; choose a route and destination based on the known landslide threat.
- ❑ Monitor NOAA Weather Radio and news broadcasts for emergency updates.
- ❑ Top off your vehicle's fuel tank with stored fuel.
- ❑ Landslides can potentially destroy your home. Prepare your evacuation vehicle by packing the 8 Ps of evacuation.
- ❑ Secure all doors and windows.
- ❑ Turn off all utilities including gas, electricity, and water.
- ❑ Before crossing bridges over waterways, check whether there is a landslide approaching, as landslides follow valleys and river catchments. If you see one, remain on your side of the bridge and move out of its path.
- ❑ Move out of the area and the landslide's potential path speedily, as the landslide will gain momentum once it starts.
- ❑ Avoid traveling through river valleys and low-lying areas, as these are more likely to be affected by landslides.
- ❑ Never drive across flooded rivers, and watch for flood debris, collapsed roads, or broken bridges. Find alternative routes if you encounter these obstacles.

NUCLEAR BLAST AND FALLOUT

When a nuclear bomb detonates, it produces a nuclear blast. The atomic reaction creates an intense pulse of heat, light, pressure, and radiation that vaporizes everything in the vicinity. A huge, mushroom-shaped fireball rises skyward. This contains radioactive materials, as well as elements that were vaporized. As the fireball cools, particles of radioactive dust form. When these descend, they create fallout, which can be dispersed over long distances by the wind, affecting places far from the blast site.

People in the immediate vicinity are killed. Those farther away may experience burst eardrums, lung injuries, and internal bleeding. Collapsing buildings and flying objects further injure people and animals. The extreme heat of the blast ignites several fires, unleashing a firestorm. Those in underground shelters may die from lack of oxygen and carbon monoxide poisoning. There would very likely be no humanitarian response, as first responders and physicians would be unable to approach radioactively contaminated areas. Relief efforts would quickly be overwhelmed.

Immediate Action

Federal and national emergency responses would be activated after a nuclear blast. Do the following immediately after a warning is issued:

- Enter the nearest building as soon as you receive the warning (outdoor areas, mobile homes, and vehicles will not provide adequate shelter). Shelter in the basement or in the middle of the building away from windows. This should protect you from the blast, heat, and radiation. Don't go onto the roof.
- Bring pets inside.
- If you are outside and cannot reach a building fast enough, shelter behind any object that might protect you. Lie down on your stomach and remain there until the blast wave has passed over. If you are stranded in a vehicle, stop and duck down.

- The fallout will begin 10–15 minutes after the blast wave has passed, so enter a building or adequate shelter as soon as possible to protect yourself.
- Do not fetch your children from school or your spouse from work, as there won't be enough time to get there and back before fallout occurs. Schools, campuses, and workplaces should have their own safety measures.
- Communication and television networks, cell phones, and the Internet will likely be disrupted. Have a NOAA-capable battery-operated or hand-crank radio available to receive news broadcasts and information.
- If you were outside during the explosion, remove your outer clothing, which could be contaminated. Shower or wash thoroughly to remove radioactive particles from your skin and hair. Alternatively, wipe down any exposed areas of your body with a damp cloth. Don't use body lotion, shampoo, or face cream, as these can bind with radioactive particles that might be on your skin.
- Stay inside for at least 24 hours or until authorities provide alternative instructions.
- Clean pets by gently brushing their hair and washing them with soap and water to remove particles.
- Avoid eating food or liquids that were outdoors at the time, although packaged foods and water may be consumed.
- If you are injured or sick, listen for instructions concerning where to receive medical attention, as well as safe exit routes.

Survival Decisions: GO

Factors supporting evacuation from your current location after a nuclear blast include:

- The structure you are in is severely damaged and dangerous.
- The structure you are in is not suitable for protecting you from radioactive fallout, such as an RV, mobile home, or other vehicle.
- You can get to a safer place in under 10 minutes.
- You do not have adequate supplies such as food, water, and medicine to survive one or two days of isolated survival.

✓ Checklist for Safe and Effective Evacuation

Note that any evacuation done immediately after a nuclear blast should be done only to take better shelter. The goal is to evacuate to a safer destination in under 10 minutes to avoid contact with nuclear fallout. Also keep in mind that there may be another nuclear blast on the way. Once radiation levels are safer (several hours to several days), there will be larger-scale evacuation procedures. Following is the best type of shelter to protect from both a nuclear blast and the resulting fallout.

❏ Shelter in a building with thick walls.

❏ Shelter in lower levels or basements if possible.

❏ Shelter in the center of buildings, away from exterior doors and windows.

❏ Locate the area of a building that is farthest from radioactive fallout with the most structure between you and the fallout.

Survival Decisions: STAY

Factors supporting staying in current location after a nuclear blast include:

- The structure you are in is not severely damaged and dangerous.
- The structure you are in is suitable for protecting you from radioactive fall-out (described earlier).
- You have adequate supplies such as food, water, and medicine to survive one or two days of isolated survival.

✓ Checklist for Safe and Effective Staying

❏ Move into a shelter as soon as an emergency is declared.

❏ Switch off air-conditioning, fans, and any other equipment that brings air into the building from outside. Shut and lock doors and windows. Close fireplace dampers.

❏ Using plastic sheeting and duct tape, seal up the doors of your shelter, as well as windows and vents so that fallout from the blast cannot enter. After the fallout cloud has passed, remove these to ventilate the room.

❏ Plan to shelter in place for at least 24 hours. Radiation exposure can decrease as much as 80 percent after a 24-hour period.

❏ Monitor news and information networks to establish when you will be able to leave. Don't leave until the authorities give the all clear.

PANDEMIC

A pandemic is a disease outbreak that affects all the world's countries, while an epidemic affects only a single city or region. Pandemics occur when a highly contagious bacterium or virus, such as COVID-19, spreads rapidly through the population. New virus strains, antibiotic-resistant pathogens, and zoonotic viruses that spread from animals to people may all create pandemics. One of the hallmarks of a pandemic is that it is sparked by a novel pathogen.

Pandemics place tremendous strain on global healthcare systems. Their effects are experienced throughout the entire healthcare system, not only in sectors dealing with critical care or infectious disease treatments. Medical supply chains may also be disrupted by lockdowns, quarantines, and other restrictions. Additionally, pandemics have a detrimental impact on economies across the globe due to lockdowns and trade restrictions.

Immediate Action

Using COVID-19 as a benchmark, here's what to do when a pandemic is declared. These recommendations may vary depending on the type of pandemic:

- Wash your hands regularly with soap and water for at least 20 seconds, ensuring that you include the back of your hands and between your fingers.
- Avoid touching your nose and mouth.
- With a dilute bleach solution, clean and disinfect any surfaces or objects you touch or use regularly. Make this solution by diluting 5 teaspoons of 5–9 percent active sodium hypochlorite bleach with 1 gallon of water.
- Follow the guidance of your primary care physician, who knows your health history and who will be receiving information from multiple sources.
- Avoid contact with people who are sick from whatever is causing the pandemic.

- Do not be around other people if you feel sick, are symptomatic, or have been exposed to the illness.
- Open doors and windows to improve ventilation and ensure that your air filtration systems work optimally.
- Use technology to stay connected to your loved ones if personal contact is prohibited or has to be avoided.
- Take care of your mental health by doing hobbies and activities you enjoy. Becoming more involved with your faith-based community can have a positive effect on your mental health as well.
- Spend time outdoors.
- Take special care of your health by eating nutritious foods, exercising, having good hygiene, and sleeping.

Survival Decisions: GO

During a pandemic, authorities generally recommend sheltering in place. However, if you need to evacuate during a pandemic, follow the guidelines of one of the previously detailed disasters that closest matches the reason for evacuation. Following is a list of pandemic-specific items you may want to consider including in your bug out bag in addition to your existing first aid kit:

- N95 face masks
- Soap
- Sanitizing wipes, gels, or sprays
- Any medicines related to treating symptoms of infection
- Extra pairs of disposable gloves
- Thermometer to monitor fevers
- Extra water for hydration, washing, and personal hygiene

Survival Decisions: STAY

It is normally recommended to shelter in place during a pandemic. However, doing so can negatively impact your mental health and physical well-being. For many, staying in place for an uncertain amount of time can be stressful, confusing, and demoralizing. This is especially true for children. Following are some actions to take to help reduce these effects. These actions apply to all scenarios where sheltering in place may be necessary.

- Eat healthy, nutritious foods.
- Exercise regularly.
- Set a schedule. Predictable routines provide a great deal of comfort to children in stressful situations.
- Engage in positive activities such as doing beloved hobbies, watching uplifting movies, or playing an instrument or a family board game.
- Spend time together rather than alone.
- Limit access to digital devices and social media platforms and encourage real social interaction.
- Only sparingly watch the news, as nearly all media reporting is fear mongering for ratings.
- Establish set jobs, chores, and responsibilities for each person and carve out time in each day to do them.
- Help someone else by mowing lawns, clearing debris, delivering food, and talking to people who live alone. Even if you can't be close to neighbors for pandemic reasons, there are still ways to make them feel loved and cared for. Engaging in this type of activity is also good for you and your children.

RIOT AND CIVIL UNREST

Riots occur when groups of aggrieved people who have a dispute engage in a violent protest. These often lead to property damage, vandalism, and personal injury. Police usually perform riot control when unrest breaks out. Riots can also be triggered by natural disasters when resources are low.

Civil unrest is an attempt to disrupt the social order by protesting or striking, either violently or peacefully. When people wish to draw attention to a real or perceived injustice, civil unrest often results.

Immediate Action

The best form of protection is to stay away from the affected area. Monitor the news and social media for details if rioting or civil unrest is threatened or begins unfolding. Never drive into a rioting group—emotions run high, and you could be pulled from your vehicle and physically attacked. However, it is possible to be caught in the wrong place at the wrong time.

If you are driving and see a protest occurring:

- Turn off the road as soon as possible, ensuring that the new route isn't a dead end.
- If you turn a corner and enter a riot, stay calm.
- Lock your doors, drive slowly, and keep vehicle revs down so that you attract less attention.
- Choose a side street and carefully maneuver out of the crowd. Never drive through a crowd.
- If you can't drive off, then park, lock your vehicle, and walk away to take shelter in the nearest safe location.
- If the crowd sets upon you quickly, drive to the side of the road and lock your doors.

If you are walking and you encounter a riot:

- Remain calm, as the demonstrators might mistake you for another protester. Mingle with the crowd and walk discreetly with them.
- Gradually work your way to the edge of the mob and walk off when you see a potential exit. Don't run, as this will draw the rioters' attention.
- Avoid being squeezed against a fence or wall or in a dead-end street, where you could be trapped and become a target.
- If the crowd is dense, avoid shop windows and glass doors, remain on your feet, and move with the crowd until you are able to break away.
- Should you be mistaken for a protester by police, stay calm and do as they say. At the police station, show them your identification. In a foreign country, request that they contact your embassy or company.

If you are at home, do the following:

- Monitor the news, text messages, and safety networks for your town.
- Secure and lock your garage and outbuildings, as well as your property's entrance gates.
- Lock all of your home's doors and stay inside. Bring in your pets.
- Make sure your cell phone is on and adequately charged.
- Check in with neighbors, relatives, and friends.

If rioters enter your property or neighborhood:

- Keep away from windows and glass doors, as ricocheting bullets or missiles such as thrown bricks or rocks are a potential hazard.
- Enter a safe room with your family members and lock the door. Remain there until the emergency has passed.
- Alternatively, enter a windowless area such as a utility room. Close and lock internal doors. Lie down to protect yourself from flying bullets.
- Alternatively, lie down on the floor and crawl underneath furniture such as a bed, large table, or desk. Keep below the windows so that you cannot be seen.

- Monitor emergency networks and move only when it is safe to do so.
- Do not engage a crowd, especially one wielding firearms, even if you have firearms training and are prepared for self-defense. Choosing to not escalate the already charged emotions of a crowd is often the best course of action.

Survival Decisions: GO

Factors supporting evacuating your home during a riot include:

- You have a medical emergency or something similar that requires evacuation.
- Your home has been invaded by the mob.

✓ Checklist for Safe and Effective Evacuation

- ❑ Implement Family Communications Plan.
- ❑ Implement evacuation plan.
- ❑ Pack some of the 8 Ps of evacuation. The most important are people, personal needs, prescriptions/first aid kit, papers, priceless items, and pets.
- ❑ Lock your home and set the alarm. Secure any sheds or garages.
- ❑ Monitor news about the riot.
- ❑ Drive *away* from your city to the outskirts of town. Riots tend to make their ways to downtown areas.

Survival Decisions: STAY

Sheltering in place is normally recommended during civil unrest. Factors supporting staying home during a riot include:

- Homes are less likely to be targeted than businesses and/or government buildings.

✓ Checklist for Safe and Effective Staying

❏ Monitor the news, social media, and security networks for your suburb or town.

❏ Stick security film on your windows so that rioters can't see inside. This will also prevent the windows from shattering so that people can't get in through them.

❏ Make sure your cell phone is on and charged. Keep it with you at all times.

❏ Carry a face mask to protect your nose and mouth from smoke, tear gas, or pepper spray. Eyeglasses will protect your eyes.

❏ Stock up on sufficient food, water, medication, and other provisions beforehand so that you don't need to go out during the event.

❏ Have your first aid kit ready.

❏ Prepare your safe room if you have one.

❏ Ensure that your smoke detectors are in good working order and you have a fire extinguisher available.

❏ Bring in outdoor furniture, propane grills, and other items that could be used by protesters to break into your home or outbuildings.

❏ Ensure that your vehicle's gas tank is topped off in case you need to evacuate or if gas stations or delivery vehicles are targeted during the unrest.

❏ Prepare your evacuation vehicle by packing the 8 Ps of evacuation.

❏ Have lethal/nonlethal weapons at the ready so that you can defend yourself if intruders get into your home.

❏ Speak to out-of-area friends, relatives, or family and make arrangements to stay with them if you need to evacuate.

❏ Prepare to have your pets indoors with you.

TERRORIST ATTACK

Terrorism is when a group or individual uses violence to force and intimidate other individuals or society to conform to a different belief system or political ideology. Attacks happen unexpectedly, giving the terrorists the advantage of surprise. Vulnerable groups are often targeted. Terrorism takes many forms and uses several methods, from biological agents, explosions, and violence to cyber-attacks and sabotage. The aim is to disrupt and frighten the community. You can also encounter terrorist attacks while traveling.

Terrorist attacks often cause numerous casualties and damage buildings and infrastructure. If your neighborhood or community is directly affected, health and medical facilities may rapidly become strained. There may be extensive media coverage of the event and disruption to workplaces, schools, campuses, and travel. You may need to evacuate your home and workplace for an indeterminate time. Cleanup after the disaster might be extensive and time-consuming.

Immediate Action

When a terrorist attack occurs, remain calm and take the following actions:

- Implement your Family Communications Plan.
- There may be additional attacks. Stay vigilant and be aware of your surroundings.
- Follow directions given by officials and monitor news broadcasts.
- Locate your first aid kit and prepare to help people.
- Provide the authorities with as much information as you can.
- Depending on the type of attack, utilities may be disrupted. Check to make sure there are no water leaks, gas leaks, or electrical shorts. If any is confirmed or suspected, turn off the corresponding utility or unplug the electronic device.
- Secure and control your pets, if applicable.

If the attack is an explosion:

- Be aware of structural damage, fires, or falling objects when navigating your home.
- Avoid elevators where applicable.
- Grab your bug out bag and evacuate as fast as possible.

Survival Decisions: GO

Factors supporting evacuation during a terrorist attack include:

- Your home is in the direct path of the attack or otherwise susceptible to damage.
- Authorities have issued an evacuation order.
- You know of or see suspicious activity.
- Post-attack hazards such as chemical exposure or water pollutants exist.

✔ Checklist for Safe and Effective Evacuation

❑ If you hear screams, gunshots, or the sounds of an explosion, establish where they are coming from and whether you are at risk. If you decide that there is a potential threat, leave immediately and don't second-guess yourself. Most of us have an intuition that warns us when something is wrong. Get others to leave with you but don't coerce them.

❑ Take your cell phone with you but don't go back for it if you happen to leave it behind. Abandon your belongings, shopping, or other items.

❑ Wherever possible, use the building's main entrances and staircases, as these are wider and easier to find than smaller exits and stairways. If the terrorists are blocking obvious exits, then you will need to use alternatives. Avoid elevators.

❑ If you are hiding because it was unsafe to leave when the attack started, wait for a break—when the terrorists are reloading, for example—and use one of the exits you previously identified. Make sure doing so will not alert them to your presence or bring you toward them.

❑ Terrorists sometimes plan a follow-up attack nearby. Bullets can travel about a mile to a target, so it's best to leave the area speedily.

- ❏ Don't hesitate at the entrance to a building or on the sidewalk, as you may impede rescue efforts or become a target. Avoid being in the open. Put taller buildings or structures between you and the terrorists.
- ❏ If law enforcement asks for a statement, give them concise, relevant details that can assist them in identifying the terrorists or their methods.

Survival Decisions: STAY

Factors supporting staying during a terrorist attack include:

- You are unable to escape.
- There are mobility issues with someone in your party.
- It is too dangerous to leave the premises due to the aftermath of an explosion.

✓ Checklist for Safe and Effective Staying

- ❏ Shelter behind the sturdiest obstacle available, preferably a load-bearing wall or concrete wall. Stay away from windows and glass.
- ❏ Have a fire extinguisher at the ready.
- ❏ Assemble the 8 Ps of evacuation while waiting if possible to do safely.
- ❏ Lie down to present as small a target as possible. Ricocheting bullets, falling objects or masonry, and fire are additional potential hazards. Listen to ascertain what is happening. Leave if there is a lull or as soon as it is safe to do so.
- ❏ Even if you can't find a sturdy obstacle to shelter behind, find a hiding place. Barricade yourself in with whatever is nearby. Communicate wirelessly with officials and wait for rescue. Keep your eyes and ears open, as the situation can escalate. The attack might be multifaceted, so be prepared to move if the terrorists approach or there are further explosions or developments near you. If you can escape safely at any stage, then leave fast.
- ❏ When you have escaped and are safe, dial 911.

TORNADO

Tornadoes form when cold, dry air meets warm, humid air, causing an updraft and creating a massive thunderstorm. If the winds suddenly change, the updraft starts rotating, fueled by more warm air and increasing in speed. Water droplets inside form a funnel cloud that grows and descends and becomes a tornado upon reaching the ground.

Tornadoes are accompanied by damaging hail and greenish skies and are particularly destructive natural forces. They are categorized in severity from F0 to F5, depending on the wind speed. Flying debris is the main cause of injuries or death during tornadoes.

The environmental impact and risks of tornadoes include:

- Pollution from airborne dust
- Broken pipelines, bunkers, and storage containers leaking pollutants, such as chemicals, oil, gas, raw sewage, and medical waste, into the affected area
- Human injuries and deaths
- Destruction of vegetation
- Topsoil removal
- Flash flooding
- Wildlife deaths and habitat loss

In the United States, most tornadoes occur in the Great Plains, with Tornado Alley—commonly including Kansas, Nebraska, Oklahoma, Texas, South Dakota, and eastern Colorado—being notorious. Around three-quarters of the world's tornadoes occur in the United States. There are often inadequate early warning systems.

Immediate Action

A tornado watch means that weather favoring tornado development is likely and people should be on alert. When a tornado appears on weather radar or is sighted, a warning is issued. Take shelter immediately. Tornado-prone areas use sirens, so know the difference between your local watch and warning sirens.

Alerts are issued via NOAA Weather Radio and text messages. According to the CDC, dark, greenish skies; a distinctive funnel cloud; a dense debris mass; large hail; and a loud roar accompany tornadoes.

If you are inside your home, school, or another building, the safest place is underground in a basement, storm cellar, or windowless room on the lowest floor—a closet, bathroom, or central hallway. If you have stairs, you can shelter underneath them, as long as there are no windows. Stairs are weight-bearing and should protect you from falling objects and debris. If possible, seek shelter under a sturdy table at the innermost part of the area.

If you are in a vehicle, mobile home, RV, or something similar, these are not safe and will not withstand the force of a tornado. Evacuate immediately to a nearby solid structure, building, or shelter designed for protection against a tornado.

If you happen to be outside, lie face down in a low, flat location such as a ditch and cover your head with your hands. Flying debris causes most fatalities during a tornado, and this is the safest type of location. Do not shelter under an overpass or a bridge.

Survival Decisions: GO

The authorities will decide whether your community should be evacuated, but there is rarely time for evacuation to make sense. By the time a tornado is spotted, the best action is to take immediate shelter. However, authorities will inform you using television or radio broadcasts, telephone calls, loudspeakers, or sirens. If your home or building lies in a floodplain or low-lying area, you might need to evacuate. Follow official instructions and evacuate quickly. Avoid driving in flooded areas and keep away from downed power lines.

Factors supporting evacuation during a tornado include:

- Your location is not suitable to withstand a tornado (lacks solid construction).
- Authorities recommend evacuation.
- There is a safer location nearby.

- There is no risk of being hit by flying debris outside.
- You are in the direct path of a tornado.
- You are not prepared to be cut off from utilities, food, water, and medical help for an undetermined amount of time.

✔ Checklist for Safe and Effective Evacuation

- ❏ Implement your Family Communications Plan.
- ❏ Implement your evacuation plan.
- ❏ Prepare your evacuation vehicle by packing the 8 Ps of evacuation.
- ❏ If you do not own a vehicle, connect with your previously chosen mode of transport.
- ❏ Unplug all electronics. Refrigerators and freezers can also be unplugged if flooding is a risk.
- ❏ Secure all doors and windows.
- ❏ Turn off utilities.
- ❏ Wear sturdy, protective shoes and clothing and a hat. Pack rain gear.
- ❏ Top off your vehicle's gas tank with stored fuel.

Survival Decisions: STAY

Factors supporting staying in place during a tornado include:

- Your location is suitable to withstand a tornado (has solid construction).
- You don't have enough time to evacuate.
- There are no safer locations to evacuate to.
- Exposure to flying debris is more dangerous than staying inside.
- Authorities recommend staying in place (only if their reasoning makes sense).

✓ Checklist for Safe and Effective Staying

❏ Go inside immediately with your pets and enter your storm shelter, cellar, or basement or a windowless room on the lowest floor. In a multistory building, go to the basement or lowest floor.

❏ Bring your bug out bag, critical documents, and as many of the 8 Ps of evacuation that you have time to assemble.

❏ Ensure that external doors are secured and locked. Close internal doors, blinds, and curtains and keep them closed.

❏ Lie or crouch on the floor. Cradle your head and neck in your arms and place blankets, cushions, and furniture around your body. Lie underneath a sturdy piece of furniture if possible.

❏ Stay indoors, avoiding windows and glass doors.

❏ If you become trapped, cover your mouth with a cloth or mask to avoid inhaling dust. Bang on a pipe or wall or whistle to attract attention. Send a text if networks are working.

❏ Monitor emergency information from authorities on NOAA Weather Radio or NOAA-compatible two-way radios. Do not leave before the all clear.

WILDFIRE

Wildfires are uncontrolled fires that burn across natural vegetation. Thousands of them consume millions of acres across the United States annually. Although fires can start naturally, most result from human carelessness or arson. Fuel loads, weather, and topography determine wildfire intensity, together with the rapidity of its spread. Uncontrolled wildfires encroaching on human habitation can be lethal.

Smoke is the most visible impact of wildfires, drifting over vast areas and affecting people miles away. Smoke contains minute particles, called particulates, that contribute to asthma, strokes, and heart attacks. Children exposed to smoke develop respiratory ailments. Fires release carbon monoxide, a gas that inhibits the body's ability to absorb oxygen, causing dizziness, headaches, and nausea.

Immediate Action

When a wildfire is nearby or approaching your community, stay calm and do the following:

- Monitor the news and your NOAA Weather Radio to receive updates and emergency information.
- Implement your Family Communications Plan by getting in touch with all family.
- Keep all windows and doors closed, including the garage door.
- If you have time, move anything flammable away from exterior house walls, including outdoor furniture, propane grills, firewood, and other debris.
- Prepare for evacuation and begin to assemble the elements of your evacuation plan.

If the fire approaches your home or community:

- Call 911 or your local emergency number immediately.
- Cover air vents and any other openings using duct tape.
- Remove all curtains and window blinds and place furniture in the center of rooms.
- Pack your vehicle with the 8 Ps of evacuation.
- Turn off your home's gas and pilot lights.
- Switch off air-conditioning.
- Attach garden hoses to outside faucets to prepare for extinguishing fires if necessary.
- Place a ladder reaching to the roof in front of the house for yourself or firefighters.
- Continue monitoring the news and NOAA Weather Radio for updates.
- Prepare to evacuate quickly if necessary.

Survival Decisions: GO

Factors supporting evacuation during a wildfire include:

- Authorities issue an evacuation order.
- You are located near an approaching wildfire.
- You have not taken advance measures to mitigate wildfire impact.
- There are limited escape routes, so it might be wise to evacuate early just in case the wildfire blocks those already limited routes.
- Someone in your home is especially vulnerable to inhaling particulates (e.g., has asthma).
- You are not prepared to be cut off from utilities, food, water, and medical help for an undetermined amount of time.

✓ Checklist for Safe and Effective Evacuation

❏ Implement your Family Communications Plan.

❏ Implement your evacuation plan; choose a route and destination based on wildfire activity.

❏ Top off your vehicle's fuel tank with stored fuel.

❏ Prepare your evacuation vehicle by packing the 8 Ps of evacuation.

❏ If you do not own a vehicle, connect with your previously chosen mode of transport.

❏ Secure all doors and windows.

❏ Turn off the gas. Leave on water and electricity.

❏ Turn on exterior lights so that your home is more visible to firefighters at night or in heavy smoke.

❏ Wear sturdy, protective shoes and clothing and a hat.

❏ Remove the debris/particulate mask from your bug out bag or first aid kit and wear it.

❏ Grab woolen blankets for potential protection since they are more fire-retardant.

❏ Roll up car windows and close air vents so that smoke doesn't enter the vehicle.

❏ Turn on your headlights.

❏ Drive away from the fire and the direction it is heading; stay on wide roads that won't become congested if many people are evacuating.

❏ Avoid downed power lines.

❏ Never drive through a wildfire.

Survival Decisions: STAY

Factors supporting staying in place during a wildfire include:

- There are no clear routes.
- Authorities recommend staying in place (only if their reasoning makes sense).
- You have made advance wildfire preparations and the space around your home is clear of vegetation and combustibles, and the building does not have wooden shingles or sidings.
- Someone in your party is especially vulnerable to smoke or particulates, so it might make more sense to keep them inside a protected environment.

✓ Checklist for Safe and Effective Staying

❏ Turn off propane or natural gas, air conditioners, fans, and equipment that circulates air around the house.

❏ Wet the roof and yard with a sprinkler or garden hose to protect from falling embers.

❏ Move flammable furniture away from windows and outer walls.

❏ Shelter in a hallway or room farthest from the fire. Avoid perimeter walls.

❏ Be sure to have your bug out bag with you, as well as a cell phone, fire extinguisher, battery-powered radio, ample water, and flashlight with extra batteries.

❏ Stay calm. Remain inside.

If you have time, consider any of the following actions to mitigate the effects of a wildfire:

❑ Trim existing trees around your home so that branches don't touch one another; also remove branches 15 feet or lower to the ground to prevent a ground fire from climbing to the tree line.

❑ Place any firewood or stacked wood at least 200 feet from the home.

❑ Clear flammable vegetation (e.g., dried leaves and pine needles, dry grass, bits of timber) from at least 100 feet around your home.

❑ Create intentional fire breaks like gravel paths or driveways to stop fires from spreading.

❑ Use fire-resistant landscaping media such as gravel rather than wood chips.

❑ Keep flammable outdoor furniture, propane grills, and similar items away from the home when they're not in use.

❑ Use fire-retardant roofing materials such as tiles, slate, pressure-treated shingles, or shakes.

❑ Make sure you have multiple smoke alarms on each floor of the home.

❑ Install fire sprinklers if possible.

❑ Purchase fire extinguishers.

❑ Keep decks, porches, gutters, and eaves clear of leaves and debris.

❑ Ensure that your garden hose has enough length to reach every part of your home and yard.

WINTER STORM

While waking up to a winter wonderland might seem attractive, winter storms also bring arctic conditions. Winter storms include snowstorms, blizzards, and—near the Great Lakes—lake effect snow conditions, which bring sleet, freezing rain, and heavy snowfalls. Blizzards occur when 35 mph winds lift snow off the ground, generating poor visibility and snowdrifts. Supercooled, freezing rain creates ice storms that coat surfaces, plants, and utility lines with layers of ice. This makes walking and driving hazardous and damages infrastructure and tree branches.

Severe winter storms have many negative impacts. The intense cold may cause frostbite and hypothermia. Heavy snowfalls may block roads and hamper deliveries and disrupt medical and emergency services. Communications and transport may be impacted, with increased road accidents. Roofs, power lines, and trees may collapse, exposing people to the cold and damaging property.

Immediate Action

A winter storm advisory means that winter conditions are not expected to be life-threatening. A winter storm watch gives you within 48 hours to prepare. If a winter storm warning is issued, then 5 or 6 or more inches of snow are expected within 12 hours and 7 or 8 inches or more within 24 hours, while a blizzard warning means that the whiteout could last 3 or more hours.

When a winter storm is nearby or approaching your community, stay calm and do the following:

- Monitor the news and NOAA Weather Radio to receive updates and emergency information.
- Implement your Family Communications Plan.
- Follow the instructions of emergency officials.
- Minimize outdoor activities.

- Drive only when strictly necessary—if you are trapped while driving, stay in your vehicle to improve your chances of being found.
- Prepare for staying in place or evacuation (details follow).

Survival Decisions: STAY

Factors supporting staying in place during a winter storm include:

- Your home is well equipped to deal with cold temperatures and power outages.
- You have backup heat sources in place.
- You've made advance preparations to shelter in place without access to food, water, power, and medical facilities for an undetermined period of time.
- Routes are blocked.
- Travel has become dangerous due to snow or ice.

✓ Checklist for Safe and Effective Staying

❏ Monitor NOAA Weather Radio and news broadcasts for emergency information.

❏ Use as few rooms as possible to conserve heat.

❏ Keep pets indoors.

❏ If venturing outside, dress in layers of loose-fitting, lightweight clothing, ensuring that your outer garments are water- and wind-repellent. Wear a hat, gloves, and sturdy waterproof boots and cover your nose and mouth with a neckerchief or gaiter.

❏ Wrap pipes in insulation or set up backup heat sources nearby. Leave the faucet on and trickle warm water through to prevent freezing.

❏ If your pipes freeze, turn on the faucets fully, remove the insulation, and heat the pipes with a backup heat source; hair dryer; or warm, damp towels. Do not use open flames on PEX or PVC pipes. Be very careful of using open flames around insulation material as it could quickly cause a house fire.

- ❏ Use generators, grills, and camp stoves in a dry, well-ventilated area.
- ❏ When you can go out, check that your gas furnace vent is not blocked by snow. This could cause carbon monoxide to backflow into the home.
- ❏ Be cautious using heaters and fireplaces. Keep all flammable materials at least 15 feet away.
- ❏ Avoid using candles, which are a fire risk.
- ❏ Eat to maintain energy levels so that your body generates heat.
- ❏ Drink sufficient warm drinks, as cold air is very drying.
- ❏ Watch for hypothermia and frostbite.

If the power goes out:

- ❏ Move to one central room and cover the windows with blankets and/or window films to maintain heat.
- ❏ Keep refrigerator and freezer doors closed.
- ❏ Monitor medication that needs refrigeration.
- ❏ Disconnect electronics and appliances to avoid damage if there are spikes when power returns.
- ❏ Use backup heat options such as space heaters or a wood stove.
- ❏ Dress for cold temperatures with multiple layers of loose-fitting clothing.
- ❏ Prepare a group sleeping area to share heat.

Survival Decisions: GO

Factors supporting evacuation during a winter storm (which is rare) include:

- Your home becomes very cold during an extended power outage.
- You have a medical or other emergency.
- Your area is at risk of flooding.

✓ Checklist for Safe and Effective Evacuation

❏ Implement your Family Communications Plan.

❏ Implement your evacuation plan; choose a route and destination based on known storm activity.

❏ Top off your vehicle's fuel tank with stored fuel.

❏ Prepare your evacuation vehicle by packing your bug out bag, first aid kit, and communications kit. Winter storms aren't likely to destroy your home, so there is no need to pack priceless items or important papers.

❏ Pack extra blankets and bedding material just in case you become stranded in your vehicle.

❏ Secure all doors and windows.

❏ Wear full winter gear with boots, hat, and face covering.

❏ Turn on your headlights.

❏ Monitor NOAA Weather Radio and news broadcasts for emergency updates.

CONCLUSION

For the past twenty-five years, I have studied, taught, and consulted about disaster preparedness. I have interviewed dozens of disaster survivors while filming my television shows *SOS: How to Survive* and *Could You Survive? with Creek Stewart*. I have received thousands of emails and letters from customers who have implemented various preparedness strategies after having read my books, taken my in-person or online courses, or watched one of my television shows.

I have never met someone who regretted being prepared. I have never met someone who didn't benefit from being prepared when something bad happened. I can say with confidence that there is a direct correlation between someone's preparedness efforts and their level of resilience. There are never any guarantees or certainties when you face an unpredictable foe, but there is no question your odds are improved both physically and mentally.

In the previous chapters, we've covered a lot of ground. If you haven't done so already, it's now time to assess your own home's risks and vulnerabilities and take action on critical components of disaster preparedness and self-reliance, including:

- Community Network Development
- Food Storage and Management
- Water Storage, Purification, and Sourcing
- Heating and Temperature Control

- Protection and Self-Defense
- Efforts Toward True Self-Sufficiency
- Deciding Your Evacuation Location
- Preparing Your 72-Hour Disaster Survival Kit (Bug Out Bag)
- Preparing Your Means of Evacuation Transportation

Preparedness is a journey that changes with your life circumstances. You must remain flexible and fluid. So many factors can cause you to reevaluate elements of your preparedness plan. These include but are not limited to changing jobs, moving to a new home, having children, taking in a senior loved one, acquiring physical limitations or disabilities, getting sick, experiencing changes in the weather, adding a pet, and so much more. My point is that your preparedness plan will never quite be finished. It is an ever-changing part of your always evolving life.

I've had the unique opportunity to experience the value of preparedness through the feedback and stories of so many people across the globe who have taken part in my writings and teachings on the subject. I am constantly encouraged by how their efforts, great or small, have positively impacted the outcome of a wide variety of disasters they have experienced. From evacuating wildfires in Colorado and California to sheltering in place during the uncertain times of COVID-19, the total time, effort, and money invested in preparedness pays valuable dividends during unexpected times. I simply call it disaster insurance.

The Importance of Action

I can't wrap up this book without again expressing the importance of action. More knowledge does not always equal more preparedness. Knowledge must be followed by action and implementation of systems and plans. In the face of uncertainty, your preparedness can be a source of strength. Take action today to build your resilience and equip yourself for whatever challenges tomorrow may bring.

I consider myself a preparedness evangelist. I regularly encourage people to become more prepared because I know how helpful it can be when disaster strikes. I would encourage you to do the same. If the plans I've outlined in this book have helped you in any way, I'd ask that you consider sharing this book with a friend or family member. It's the gift that keeps on giving!

And would you please consider leaving a review at the site where you purchased this book? Reviews help other customers make educated decisions. I read each and every review in an effort to create new and better content in the future.

Thank you for buying this book, and I wish you resilience, a strong mind, and confidence in whatever comes your way. Remember, it's not IF but WHEN!

INDEX

about: importance of, 11–12

A.I.M. (anticipate, identify, manage) for, 12–13

combat breathing and, 13

importance of action, 245–46

Public transportation, 15–16

Purification of water. *See* Water, purifying and filtering

R

Radiation, responding to, 97, 217–20

Rain barrel, 59, 60

Ready.gov, 18

Recession/economic collapse, responding to, 184–87

Refuge Medical, 99

Relationships. *See* Community and network development

Relatives, evacuation and, 137

Resource page, link for, 22

Resources. *See specific items*

Respiratory emergencies, 97

Respiratory supports, 103. *See also* First aid *references*

Rifle, 116. *See also* Self-defense

Riot and civil unrest, responding to, 224–27

Risk assessment

about: disaster reality and, 16; overview and importance, 16

conducting, 17

data sources of potential risks, 18–19

economic exposure/vulnerability, 20, 22

exposure analysis, vulnerability evaluation, 17, 19–22

identifying risk, 17–19

neighborhood risks, 32

physical exposure/vulnerability, 20, 21

preparedness plan, 17, 23–25

reducing risk, 23

risk reduction and, 17, 23

social exposure/vulnerability, 20, 21

Risk mitigation, preparedness and, 11

Road closures, 155. *See also* Transportation

Rocket stoves, 46–49

Rocks, heating using, 65

Rotating food stores, 39

S

Scalds, burns, and radiation, 97

Security. *See also* Personal protection; Self-defense

bars on windows, sliding doors, 120–22

crime deterrents, 117

door hardware for, 119–20

door security bar, 120, 122

doorstop alarms, 118

hardening your home, 119–23

hurricane fabric for, 123

motion-activated cameras for, 118

neighborhood plan, 33–34

outdoor lights for, 117

safety and, 116–19

systems, 119

Self-defense. *See also* Personal protection; Security

about: overview of personal protection and, 109

basics, 111–16

Byrna less-lethal launcher for, 115

Castle Doctrine laws and, 111

Duty to Retreat laws and, 111

evacuation needs, 144

firearms for, 115–16

law categories, 110

martial arts training and, 113

pepper spray, mace for, 114–15

personal fitness and, 112

power in numbers, 111

self-sufficiency checklist, 128

situational awareness and, 111–12

Stand Your Ground laws and, 110

staying home and, 112

stun guns for, 113–14

tasers and, 113

weaponized personal items for, 113

Self-sufficiency in emergencies, 13–15

about: overview of, 13, 124

concept of, 125

falling short, preparing for, 131

importance of, 13, 129, 244–46

mindset for, 14, 129, 130

preparing home for (checklists), 125–29

skill sets for, 15

72-hour Backpack. *See* Bug out bags
Shelter, evacuation checklist, 142–43
Sheltering in place
    about: deciding to stay or go, 26;
      overview of, 26–27
    communication needs (*See*
      Communications)
    evacuating instead of (*See* 8 Ps of
      evacuation; Evacuation; Transportation)
    first-aid and (*See* First aid *references*)
    food and (*See* Food *references*)
    heat and (*See* Heat, off-grid options; Heat
      and temperature control)
    power concerns (*See* Power generation
      and backup)
    self-defense and (*See* Personal protection;
      Security; Self-defense)
    self-sufficiency importance, 13, 129,
      244–46 (*See also* Self-sufficiency in
      emergencies)
    specific situations and (*See* Disasters and
      emergency situations, specific responses)
    water concerns (*See* Water *references*)
Shelters, public, 139
Shock, 96
Shooter, active, responding to, 162–64
Shotgun, 116. *See also* Self-defense
Situational awareness, 111–12
Skill sets, for self-reliance, 15
Societal unrest, response examples. *See*
  Disasters and emergency situations, specific
  responses
Solar panels, 75
Solar power. *See also* Power generation and
  backup
    battery power charging station, 81–84
    panels/power stations, 75, 80
    portable generators, 80
Space heaters. *See* Heat *references*
Splinting materials, 102. *See also* First aid
  references
Stand Your Ground laws, 110. *See also*
  Self-defense

Stoves
    improvised toilet paper alcohol stove,
      65–66
    off-grid cooking/Rocket stoves, 46–49
    wood-burning stove/fireplace, 70–72
Strike plates, upgrading, 120
Strollers, carts, and wagons, 156–59
Stun guns, 113–14
Sunlight, food storage and, 37
Survival bunker, 138
Survival decisions, examples. *See* Disasters
  and emergency situations, specific
  responses

T

Tasers/stun guns, 113
Temperature, storage, 37
Terrorist attack, responding to, 228–30
Tiered neighborhood communications plan,
  31–32
Toilet paper-alcohol stove, 65–66
Toilets
    evacuation plan and, 135, 198, 199
    water from tanks, 61
Tools
    battery power bank for, 81–84
    evacuation needs, 144
Tornado, responding to, 231–34
Toxic and poisoning exposure, 97
Trailers, 155, 157
Transportation
    alternative options, 154–55
    carts, strollers and wagons, 156–59
    evacuation vehicle, 152–54
    preparing vehicle for evacuation, 153–54
    public, 15–16
    road closures, obstacles and, 155
    72-hour backpack and (*See* Bug out bags)
    trailers, 155, 157
    traveling on foot and, 156–59
Trauma and musculoskeletal injuries, 96

U

United States Geological Survey (USGS), 19
US Department of Homeland Security, 18

V

Vacation condo, evacuation to, 138
Vehicles
    cargo storage, 152–53
    distance to travel and, 153
    evacuation, 152–54
    off-road capability, 153
    preparing for evacuation, 153–54
    trailers with, 155, 157
Ventless gas heaters (propane/natural gas), 70
Violence, disaster, 110. *See also* Personal
    protection; Self-defense
Vulnerability evaluation, exposure analysis
    and, 17, 19–22. *See also* Risk assessment

W

Wagons, carts, and strollers, 156–59
Walkie-talkies, 88, 90
Walking, traveling on foot, 156–59
Walls, blanket, 66–67
War/foreign invasion, responding to,
    200–203. *See also* Fallout/nuclear blast
Warmth. *See* Heat and temperature control
Water, 50–62
    about: in disaster preparedness, 51;
        importance and safety, 50; self-reliance
        and, 15
    containers (small, medium, large), 52–54,
        55
    daily usage, 51–52
    disinfecting, 55
    drum pumps to access, 54
    evacuation needs, 143 (*See also*
        Evacuation, 8 Ps of)
    heating, 64
    quality maintenance, 55–56
    rain barrel for, 59, 60
    renewable sources, 58–60
    replacing, refreshing stores, 55
    self-sufficiency checklist, 126–27
    storage strategies/conditions, 51–54,
        55–56
    store-bought bottled water/jugs, 52
    weight considerations, 52, 54
Water, purifying and filtering

bleach purification, 61
boiling water, 60–61
gravity-fed filter, 57, 58
purification vs. filtration, 56–58
Water pipes
    draining, 24, 135
    keeping from freezing, 69, 189, 241
    unfreezing, 241
    water from, 61
Weapons. *See* Personal protection;
    Self-defense
Weather
    about: information sources, 89, 90, 94
    avalanche responses, 165–69
    extreme heat responses, 194–96
    flooding responses, 197–99
    hurricane responses, 206–9
    tornado responses, 231–34
    winter storm responses, 240–43
Weatherproofing home, 72–73
Weather stripping, 73
Wildfire, responding to, 235–39
Windows, sealing/upgrading, 72–73. *See also*
    Hurricane fabric
Winter storm, responding to, 240–43
Wood-burning stove/fireplace, 70–72
Wound care and bleeding, 96. *See also* First
    aid *references*

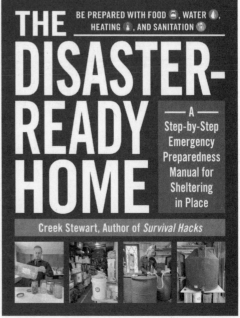